M000031566

A psalm is the work of angels, a heavenly institution, the spiritual incense. Oh! The wise invention of the teacher who contrived that while we were singing we should at the same time learn something useful; by this means, too, the teachings are in a certain way impressed more deeply on our minds . . . What, in fact, can you not learn from the psalms? Can you not learn the grandeur of courage? The exactness of justice? The nobility of self-control? The perfection of prudence? A manner of penance? The measure of patience? . . . Therein is perfect theology, a prediction of the coming of Christ in the flesh . . . a hope of resurrection . . . an unveiling of mysteries; all things, as if in some great public treasury, are stored in the Book of Psalms.

St. Basil the Great, Exegetic Homilies, 10 (1, 2)

Each of these books [of Scripture], you see, is like a garden which grows one special kind of fruit; by contrast, the Psalter is a garden which, besides its [own] special fruit, grows also some . . . of [the fruit of] all the rest.

St. Athanasius, *Letter to Marcellinus*

O Lord, Open My Lips

The Psalms in the Liturgy

DIANNE BERGANT, CSA

LITURGY
TRAINING
PUBLICATIONS

Nihil Obstat
Reverend Mr. Daniel G. Welter, JD
Chancellor
Archdiocese of Chicago
November 15, 2017

Imprimatur
Very Reverend Ronald A. Hicks
Vicar General
Archdiocese of Chicago
November 15, 2017

The *Nihil Obstat* and *Imprimatur* are declarations that the material is free from doctrinal or moral error, and thus is granted permission to publish in accordance with c. 827. No legal responsibility is assumed by the grant of this permission. No implication is contained herein that those who have granted the *Nihil Obstat* and *Imprimatur* agree with the content, opinions, or statements expressed.

Scripture texts in this work are taken from the *New American Bible*, revised edition © 2010, 1991, 1986, 1970 Confraternity of Christian Doctrine, Washington, DC, and are used by permission of the copyright owner. All Rights Reserved. No part of the *New American Bible* may be reproduced in any form without permission in writing from the copyright owner.

Excerpts from the *Lectionary for Mass for Use in the Dioceses of the United States of America*, second typical edition © 2001, 1998, 1997, 1986, 1970 Confraternity of Christian Doctrine, Inc., Washington, DC. Used with permission. All rights reserved. No portion of this text may be reproduced by any means without permission in writing from the copyright owner.

Excerpts from the General Introduction of the English translation of *The Liturgy of the Hours* © 1973, 1974, 1975, International Commission on English in the Liturgy Corporation (ICEL); excerpts from *Documents on the Liturgy, 1963–1979: Conciliar, Papal, and Curial Texts* © 1982, ICEL; excerpts from the English translation of *Rite of Christian Initiation of Adults* © 1985, ICEL; excerpts from the English translation of *The Roman Missal* © 2010, ICEL. All rights reserved. Texts contained in this work derived whole or in part from liturgical texts copyrighted by ICEL have been published here with the confirmation of the Committee on Divine Worship, United States Conference of Catholic Bishops. No other texts in this work have been formally reviewed or approved by the United States Conference of Catholic Bishops.

Excerpts from the English translation of the *Catechism of the Catholic Church* for use in the United States of America Copyright © 1994, United States Catholic Conference, Inc.—Libreria Editrice Vaticana. Used with permission.

Quotations from *Verbum Domini* and *The Interpretation of the Bible in the Church* © Libreria Editrice Vaticana.

O Lord, Open My Lips: The Psalms in the Liturgy © 2018 Archdiocese of Chicago: Liturgy Training Publications, 3949 South Racine Avenue, Chicago, IL 60609; 800-933-1800; fax 800-933-7094; e-mail: orders@ltp.org; website: www.LTP.org. All rights reserved.

This book is part of the *Liturgy and the Bible* series.

This book was edited by Lorie Simmons. Michael A. Dodd was the production editor, Anna Manhart was the designer, and Kari Nicholls was the production artist.

Cover: St. Albans Psalter. Dombibliothek Hildesheim, HS St.God. 1 (Property of the Basilica of St. Godehard, Hildesheim), p. 133; Interior: St. Albans Psalter. Dombibliothek Hildesheim, HS St.God. 1 (Property of the Basilica of St. Godehard, Hildesheim), p. 193 ; p. 15: MS Bodl. Or. 621, fol. 3a. Wikimedia Commons, Jewish Museum; pp. 30 and 44: (c) John Zich; p. 67: Matt Cashore/University of Notre Dame.

22 21 20 19 18   1 2 3 4 5

Printed in the United States of America.

Library of Congress Control Number: 2017964299

ISBN: 978-1-61671-310-2

LBOLO

CONTENTS

WELCOME TO THIS STUDY OF THE PSALMS IN THE LITURGY

The psalms are some of the Bible's most beloved texts. This book aims to help you appreciate how the liturgy enhances the role of the psalms in the lives of believers. We will begin with the wisdom of Church teaching about Scripture, especially in Pope Benedict's post-synodal apostolic exhortation *Verbum Domini: On the Word of God in the Life and Mission of the Church* (VD). Next we will discuss some of the theology contained in the psalms, particularly images of God found in these ancient hymns. These explorations will prepare us to examine the role of the psalms in the liturgy, the privileged setting for the Word of God. We will consider how the specific liturgical settings in which we encounter the psalms contribute to their meaning: the Responsorial Psalm at Mass, especially Sunday Mass, then ritual Masses (particularly those for the sacraments of Baptism of infants, Matrimony, and Anointing of the Sick), and non-Eucharistic Liturgies of the Word, as well as the psalms in the Liturgy of the Hours. Finally, we will discuss the psalms in the practice of lectio divina.

ABBREVIATIONS

CCC   *Catechism of the Catholic Church*

GILOH *General Instruction of the Liturgy of the Hours*

GIRM   *General Instruction of the Roman Missal*

SC   *Constitution on the Sacred Liturgy (Sacrosanctum Concilium)*

VD   *Verbum Domini: On the Word of God in the Life and Mission of the Church*

CHAPTER 1

The Word of God

The Church's Wisdom about Sacred Scripture

In 2008, Pope Benedict XVI convened a general assembly of the synod of bishops to discuss the importance of the Bible in the lives of believers. Following this meeting, in 2010, the Pope issued an apostolic exhortation entitled *Verbum Domini: On the Word of God in the Life and Mission of the Church*. This document reviewed the implementation of the directives found in the Second Vatican Council's *Dogmatic Constitution on Divine Revelation (Dei Verbum)*, which appeared in 1965. In *Verbum Domini*, Pope Benedict also wanted to address the challenges contemporary society sets before Christian believers.

The Council's document, *Dei Verbum*, had expressed a new insight about Sacred Scripture. Instead of seeing it as a text that only demonstrated the truth of Church doctrine or inspired devotion, the Church now saw Scripture as one of the means of God's self-revelation to human beings. Pope Benedict's document *Verbum Domini* follows this same line of thought. It consists of three parts: "Verbum Dei" ("The Word of God"), which examines the various ways God's Word is expressed to humans, including the actual text of Scripture; "Verbum in Ecclesia" ("The Word in the Church"), which summarizes the function of Scripture in the life of the Church; and "Verbum Mundo" ("The Word to the World"), which gives an overview of the role of Scripture in the broader society. The focus of this book on the role of the psalms in the liturgy is discussed in part 2 of Pope Benedict's exhortation ("The Word in the Church"). To understand this role, however, we first need to understand the nature of the psalms as Sacred Scripture and how to employ appropriate methods of interpreting them (the content of part 1 of the exhortation, "The Word of God"). We also need to appreciate the forcefulness of their meaning for the transformation of the entire world (the content of part 3, "The Word to the World"). Since Pope Benedict's apostolic exhortation sets the framework for our understanding and appreciation of Scripture generally, and the psalms in particular, in it we can find insights to enrich our grasp of the relevance and power of the psalms' religious message.

The first part of *Verbum Domini* ("The Word of God") consists of three sections. The first discusses how Scripture reveals the ways God's Word has spoken and is still speaking to us; the second treats Scripture as our response to God's speaking; and the third offers various ways of interpreting this divine communication — God's revelation and our human response to it.

God's Self-Revelation in the Psalms

Scripture is a testimony to the way our religious ancestors (the ancient Israelites and the early Christians) experienced God's self-revelation in their lives. It was through various events that they came to know what God chose to reveal to them. The geographic, social, and political circumstances within which they lived, the ways in which various aspects of their culture shaped their understanding and their behavior, and their interactions with each other and with other nations shaped the way they perceived God as active in their lives. It was through such experiences that they came to know God as a deliverer, provider, covenant partner, and ultimately as one who was revealed in human flesh.

Though the ancient biblical story seems to unfold as actual human history, and we can learn much about our religious ancestors from this unfolding story, it is really an account of their perception of God working in the world of which they were a part. Their understanding of the cosmos was God-centered:

The heavens declare the glory of God (Psalm 19:2)

as was their realization of human dignity:

> Yet you have made him [weak human beings]
>> little less than a god,
>> crowned him [them] with glory and honor.   (Psalm 8:6)

They believed that God was both far above all creation in majesty:

> Appear on high over the heavens, God;
>> your glory above all the earth;   (Psalm 108:6)

and immanently close at hand:

> LORD, you have probed me, you know me:
>> you know when I sit and stand;
>> you understand my thoughts from afar.   (Psalm 139:1–2)

Hardship was seen as punishment for infidelity, while success was considered God's blessing for their loyalty:

> Those who do evil will be cut off,
>> but those who wait for the LORD will inherit the earth.
>>>>> (Psalm 37:9)

There was no aspect of life, no event that did not bear some dimension of divine self-revelation.

In the New Testament, we read:

> In times past, God spoke in partial and various ways to our ancestors through the prophets; in these last days, he spoke to us through a son, whom he made heir of all things and through whom he created the universe. (Hebrews 1:1–2)

The entire life of this Son revealed God. The words of this Son:

> "Neither do I condemn you. Go, [and] from now on do not sin any more," (John 8:11)

and his acts of compassion:

> Moved with pity, Jesus touched their eyes, (Matthew 20:34)

echoed the divine compassion found in ancient Israelite texts. This Son employed familial language to characterize his unique relationship with God:

> "No one knows who the Son is except the Father, and who the Father is except the Son and anyone to whom the Son wishes to reveal him," (Luke 10:22)

as well as the relationship between God and those who believe:

> "You will be children of the Most High." (Luke 6:35)

Finally, this Son assured his followers that this relationship with God would endure:

> "Inherit the kingdom prepared for you from the foundation of the world." (Matthew 25:34)

These few examples from both biblical testaments demonstrate how the Scriptures testify to God's self-revelation. For believers, these same Scriptures are more than the testimonies of our religious ancestors; furthermore, they are more than traditional stories. They are also the means through which God reveals God's self to us today. What is true about Scripture generally is specifically true about the psalms. God is revealed to us today through the psalms. In fact, the fundamental theology of ancient Israel is found within the collection of psalms known as the Psalter.

Our Response to God in the Psalms

The second section of part 1 of Pope Benedict's apostolic exhortation addresses our response to the God who speaks to us. It is clear that as human testimonies of the faith of the ancient Israelites, the Scriptures are certainly a response. Yet even more important than their literary form (testimonies) is the content of those testimonies. They not only show *that* the Israelites responded to God, but also *how* they did.

Illuminated letter T from the St. Albans Psalter, made at St. Albans Abbey in England in the twelfth century. On this page illustrating Psalm 64 (65 in our modern Bibles), Christ sits in the upper part of the T, making a sign of blessing with one hand and with the other, grasping the hand of one of the psalm singers below. Adding to this expression of care and familiarity, Christ's feet rest on the man's shoulders. Two of the three men below Christ point to the first line of the psalm, signifying that they are praising Christ with those words: "A hymn, God, becomes / [befits] you in Syon, / and a vow shall be paid back to you in Jerusalem. Hear my prayer / to you all flesh shall come." The image illustrates the dynamic of the psalms in the liturgy. God reaches out and cares for us and we respond with praise and gratitude.

The primary form of response to God is worship, and many biblical passages describe forms of worship. Chief among them are expressions of prayer, and psalms are considered Israel's prayer par excellence. The Psalter comprises prayers, both individual and communal, that express profound religious sentiments of praise, lament, confidence, and gratitude. Since ancient Israel's sociopolitical structure was theocratic, many political statements might also be considered religious responses. While religious expressions related to social and political circumstances can be found in many different kinds of psalms, they are most prominent in royal or Davidic psalms. Regardless of their literary type, these prayers, and these political statements, all flowed from Israel's primary response to their self-revealing God. This primary response was Israel's acceptance of God's invitation to be God's covenant partner.

In the ancient world, covenants were serious socio-political agreements made between rulers and their people:

> Then Abner said to David, "I will now go to assemble all Israel for my lord the king, that they may make a covenant with you; you will then be king over all whom you wish to rule." (2 Samuel 3:21)

Covenants were also made between equals:

> "Come, now, let us make a covenant, you [Jacob] and I [his uncle Laban]; and it will be a treaty between you and me." (Genesis 31:44)

Such covenants carried mutual promises of protection and cooperation. Ancient Israel appropriated this practice and applied it to its relationship with God, even though it understood that this was not a covenant among equals:

> "I will maintain my covenant between me and you and your descendants after you throughout the ages as an everlasting covenant, to be your God and the God of your descendants after you." (Genesis 17:7)

Always conscious of the covenant established between their God and them, the ancient Israelites interpreted the events of their lives as evidence of the character and quality of this covenant. Peace and prosperity were seen as God's pleasure for their fidelity; misfortune was interpreted as divine displeasure in the face of their unfaithfulness. This interpretation of life situations can be seen in the religious sentiments we find in the psalms, sentiments that highlight the nature of the people's response to God's action. There we find amazement:

> O LORD, our Lord,
> > how awesome is your name through all the earth!
> > I will sing of your majesty above the heavens   (Psalm 8:2)

and praise:

> Hallelujah!
> Praise the name of the LORD!
> > Praise, you servants of the LORD.   (Psalm 135:1)

There are expressions of confidence:

> The LORD is my shepherd;
> > there is nothing I lack,   (Psalm 23:1)

and gratitude:

> We thank you, God, we give thanks;
> > we call upon your name,
> > we declare your wonderful deeds.   (Psalm 75:2)

We also find complaint:

> How long, LORD? Will you utterly forget me?
> > How long will you hide your face from me?   (Psalm 13:2)

regret:

> All day long my disgrace is before me;
> > shame has covered my face,   (Psalm 44:16)

and contrition:

> I acknowledge my guilt
> > and grieve over my sin.   (Psalm 38:19)

There are also psalms that express national loyalty:

> O God, give your judgment to the king;
>> your justice to the king's son;
> That he may govern your people with justice,
>> your oppressed with right judgment. (Psalm 72:1–2)

Other psalms extol the benefits that accrue from respect for the Law:

> The law of the LORD is perfect,
>> refreshing the soul.
> The decree of the LORD is trustworthy,
>> giving wisdom to the simple.
> The precepts of the LORD are right,
>> rejoicing the heart.
> The command of the LORD is clear,
>> enlightening the eye. (Psalm 19:8–9)

These are all examples of how the psalms functioned as responses to God's self-revelation. The psalms continue to express our own response to God as we employ them in our various forms of prayer.

Interpreting the Psalms

In 1994, an important document was published by the Pontifical Biblical Commission entitled *The Interpretation of the Bible in the Church*. In it, all methods employed for the interpretation of the Bible were explained and critiqued for their strengths and weaknesses. This included historical-critical and literary-critical methods as well as the social-scientific approaches such as liberationist and feminist interpretation. Only one approach, fundamentalist interpretation, was judged to be "dangerous, for it is attractive to people who look to the Bible for ready answers to the problems of life" (116). It is also "often anti-church," because "it considers of little importance the creeds, the doctrines and liturgical practices which have become part of church tradition, as well as the teaching function of the church itself" (115).

The many methods of biblical interpretation can be divided into three basic approaches, each attentive to a particular aspect of the actual practice of reading. One approach examines what is referred to as "the world within the text" — the world of the story, the world created by the author. This approach focuses on literary characteristics including literary form or genre (history, fiction, poetry, and so forth), and literary devices (simile, metaphor, allegory, and the like). Another approach is concerned with "the world behind the text," the actual world of the

Methods of biblical interpretation can be divided into three basic approaches.

author. Here the primary focus of examination moves away from exclusive attention to the text itself and attempts to recapture aspects of the political, social, religious, or other cultural profile of the time of its composition. This approach seeks to uncover the original meaning intended by the author. Finally, a third approach addresses "the world in front of the text," the world of the reader. In this approach the text is read through the particular experience or interest of the reader — a lens determined by the reader. Examples of such a lens could include the reader's socioeconomic experience, gender, or point of view, the reader's interest in or need for liberation from some oppressive condition — perhaps political or social, or a concern for the integrity of creation.

While all reading seeks to uncover the meaning of the text, a text can yield myriad meanings depending upon which approach is chosen. Is the meaning found in the literary creativity of the text itself? Is it found in the meaning originally intended by the author? Or does it flow from the particular interest of the reader?

A brief look at Psalm 8 from the perspectives of each of these approaches will demonstrate both the different focuses and the richness these approaches can generate.

> O Lord, our Lord,
>> how awesome is your name through all the earth!
> I will sing of your majesty above the heavens
>> with the mouths of babes and infants.

You have established a bulwark against your foes,
>   to silence enemy and avenger.
When I see your heavens, the work of your fingers,
>   the moon and stars that you set in place —
What is man that you are mindful of him,
>   and a son of man that you care for him?
Yet you have made him little less than a god,
>   crowned him with glory and honor.
You have given him rule over the works of your hands,
>   put all things at his feet:
All sheep and oxen,
>   even the beasts of the field,
The birds of the air, the fish of the sea,
>   and whatever swims the paths of the seas.
O LORD, our Lord,
>   how awesome is your name through all the earth!
>   (Psalm 8:2–10)

Literary analysis tells us that this is a psalm of praise, extolling God as Creator. It also acclaims the marvels of human beings, specifically weak, limited human beings (אנוש), who have been given some form of authority over the rest of creation. This literary approach also highlights the similarity between the list of animals in the psalm with that found in the first Genesis creation narrative (Genesis 1:26, 28).

Historical analysis, the second approach, looks at this characterization of the human beings in a significantly different way. The kind of authority suggested in both this psalm and the creation account would be seen by the ancient Israelites, from whom the psalm emerged, as referring to the way monarchy functioned in their time. Exercising rule (Psalm 8) as well as subduing and having dominion (Geneis 1) are prerogatives of royalty. However, as Genesis 1 further states, the royalty functions are bequeathed to humans because they are "images of God," representatives of the divine, not because they are autonomous deities.

Today, when choosing the third approach, readers might read the psalm through an anthropological lens and discover the profile of limited human beings who can achieve great feats. Feminists disturbed by the gender-specific language might read the psalm through a lens influenced by Genesis 1, where both the man and the woman were given the command to subdue and have dominion. Ecologists might also employ the Genesis account to interpret the psalm, for there human beings are clearly depicted as being accountable to God to ensure that all living beings can increase and multiply and thrive.

No approach alone yields everything.

Each of these three approaches yields some valuable information. However, no approach alone yields everything.

The Structure of the Psalter

Before discussing specific aspects of the psalms, we should observe the general structure of the Psalter and several literary features of many of the individual psalms. While the psalms themselves originated in various situations throughout the long history of the people of Israel, their features reveal the hand of an editor or editors. First, the one hundred fifty psalms have been divided into five "books" or collections (Psalms 1–41; 42–72; 73–89; 90–106; 107–150). These collections are divided with words of praise: "Blessed be the LORD, the God of Israel . . . " that appear in the last verse of the last psalm in each of the collections (Psalms 41:14; 72:18; 89:53; 106:48). Second, the "books" in this present organization contain psalms that belonged to earlier collections classified by presumed authors: Psalms of David (1–9; 11–41; and 51–65; among others); Psalms of Solomon (72; 127), Psalms of Asaph (50; 73–83); and Psalms of the Korahites (42; 44–49; 84–85; 87–88). Third, several psalms contain a superscription consisting of introductory words that identify the original collection from which the psalm was drawn and frequently offer some liturgical direction for public singing: "For the leader; 'upon the gittith.' A Psalm of David" (Psalm 8:1), or even suggest the historical circumstances of the psalm's origin: "Of David, when he feigned madness before Abimelech, who drove him out and he went away" (Psalm 34:1). Fourth, the word Selah is found at the end of verses in several psalms (Psalms 3:3, 5, 9; 32:4, 5, 7; 46:4, 8, 12; and so forth). Though its meaning is not certain, scholars generally consider it a directive for pausing during communal recitation. Finally, in respect for the personal name of the God of Israel, YHWH is rendered in translation as LORD, using capital letters to differentiate it from the Hebrew word, אדון, the actual word for "lord."

CHAPTER 2

The Theology of the Psalms

As already stated, ancient Israel's essential theology is expressed in its psalms. The information in this chapter fits under the category "world within the text," explained in the previous chapter. It concerns the meaning of the psalms. Sometimes this meaning is rather obvious, for it is not difficult to recognize a complaint in contrast to an expression of thanksgiving or praise. However, cultural differences might prevent us from understanding what is being said. Or, we might presume that we grasp the meaning, when it is the cultural difference itself that we misinterpret. In that case, historical information can be helpful, and that leads us to step into the "world behind the text."

While it is impossible to discuss here all aspects of this theology, four components are essential: election, deliverance and creation, integrity of creation, and the Law and wisdom.

> Cultural differences might prevent us from understanding what is being said.

Election

The most significant boast of the ancient Israelites was that they were God's "chosen people":

> For the LORD has chosen Jacob for himself,
>> Israel as his treasured possession.
>>> (Psalm 135:4; see also Psalms 33:12; 105:43; 106:5)

This conviction traces divine election all the way back to the very earliest ancestors, particularly Abraham:

> [God] remembers forever his covenant,
>> the word he commanded for a thousand generations,

> Which he made with Abraham,
>> and swore to Isaac.
>>> (Psalm 105:8–9; see also Psalms 47:10; 105:42)

This covenant was renewed with Jacob:

> But I will rejoice forever;
>> I will sing praise to the God of Jacob.
>>> (Psalm 75:10; see also Psalms 20:2; 22:24;
>>> 46:8, 12; 81:2, 5; 114:7; 146:5; and so forth)

While this ancestral aspect of the tradition has been considered by many as a feature of tribal organization, the election of David as king identified the people as a nation that was recognized in the ancient Near Eastern world. Some of Israel's national characteristics, the people believed, were ordained by God. We know how important this tradition was because of the large number of psalms belonging to the classification known as Royal Psalms (Psalms 2, 18, 21, 20, 45, 72, 101, 110, 132, 144). This is not a royal tradition in a general sense; rather, it is specific to the house of David:

> You have given great victories to your king,
>> and shown mercy to his anointed,
>>> to David and his posterity forever.   (Psalm 18:51)

> He chose David his servant,
>> took him from the sheepfolds.
> From tending ewes God brought him,
>> to shepherd Jacob, his people,
>>> Israel, his heritage.   (Psalm 78:70–71)

> I have made a covenant with my chosen one;
>> I have sworn to David my servant:
> I will make your dynasty stand forever
>> and establish your throne through all ages.   (Psalm 89:4–5)

Kings were always anointed:

> I have chosen David, my servant;
>> with my holy oil I have anointed him.   (Psalm 89:21)

Consequently, a messianic tradition (from the Hebrew word ‎משיח‎, *messiah* or *anointed one*) developed that was eventually interpreted by Christians as having been fulfilled in Jesus. The use of the psalms in Christian prayer gives them a Christological interpretation. This is particularly evident during major feasts. For example, on the Solemnity of the Body and Blood of Christ, aspects of both the idea of

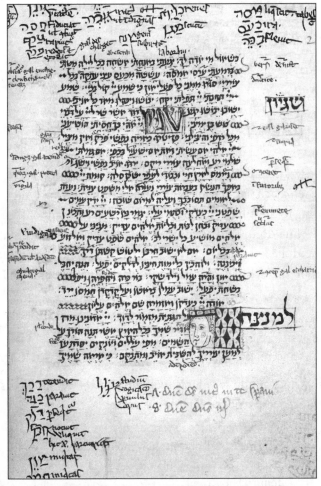

A page from a Hebrew psalter from the thirteenth century. It was used by Christian students who made notes in the margins in Latin and French. Medieval Christian scholars often consulted Hebrew works on the psalms, even as they interpreted these ancient texts from a Christian perspective. This page displays the last part of Psalm 7 and the beginning of Psalm 8.

a royal messiah and royal priesthood, which originated in ancient Israel, are attributed to Christ:

> The LORD says to my lord:
>> "Sit at my right hand,
>> while I make your enemies your footstool."
> The scepter of your might:
>> the LORD extends your strong scepter from Zion.
>> Have dominion over your enemies!
> Yours is princely power from the day of your birth.
>> In holy splendor before the daystar,
>>> like dew I begot you.
>
> The LORD has sworn and will not waver:
>> "You are a priest forever in the manner of Melchizedek."
>
> (Psalm 110:1–4)

Every ancient Near Eastern king was expected to have an impressive palace. Furthermore, it was required that a temple, corresponding to the king's palace, be constructed in honor of the major god of the kingdom. The monarchy was responsible for building this temple, and the king frequently enjoyed a prominent role in the cult practiced in that temple. This certainly was the case in ancient Israel:

> Three times a year Solomon used to offer burnt offerings and
> communion offerings on the altar which he had built to the LORD,
> and to burn incense before the LORD.
>> Thus he completed the temple. (1 Kings 9:25)

Several psalms allude to temple worship and the religious dispositions required to participate in that worship:

> LORD, who may abide in your tent?
>> Who may dwell on your holy mountain?
> Whoever walks without blame,
>> doing what is right,
>> speaking truth from the heart;
> Who does not slander with his tongue,
>> does no harm to a friend,
>> never defames a neighbor;

Who disdains the wicked,
>> but honors those who fear the LORD;
>> Who keeps an oath despite the cost,
>> lends no money at interest,
>> accepts no bribe against the innocent
Whoever acts like this
>> shall never be shaken. (Psalm 15:1–5)

Who may go up the mountain of the LORD?
>> Who can stand in his holy place?
"The clean of hand and pure of heart,
>> who has not given his soul to useless things,
>> what is vain." (Psalm 24:3–4)

It is clear that while election was initiated by God, it carried a consequence: the responsibility on the part of individuals. This was particularly true with regard to Davidic election. David and his household were chosen, but this choice required political and military protection and leadership as well as religious obligations. The national yet royal temple became the center of the religious life of the people. It was primarily there that they confirmed their election by God. Evidence of this is found in a collection of psalms identified in their superscriptions as "Songs of Ascent" (Psalms 120–134), which were probably sung by pilgrims as they approached Jerusalem during the time of the major religious festivals.

Deliverance and Creation

The most important event in the history of the ancient Israelite people was their deliverance from Egyptian bondage. According to them, this was evidence, par excellence, of their special election by God. In fact, one of the oldest pieces of poetry found in the Bible contains a hymn that praises God for this deliverance (Exodus 15:1–12). Similar praise is found in many of the psalms:

>> He changed the sea to dry land;
>> through the river they passed on foot. (Psalm 66:6)

He split the sea and led them across,
    making the waters stand like walls.   (Psalm 78:13)

He led them on secure and unafraid,
    while the sea enveloped their enemies.   (Psalm 78:53)

He roared at the Red Sea and it dried up.
    He led them through the deep as through a desert.
                                                    (Psalm 106:9)

Who split in two the Red Sea,
    for his mercy endures forever . . .
    But swept Pharaoh and his army into the Red Sea,
    for his mercy endures forever.   (Psalm 136:13, 15)

It is in this tradition of deliverance that we find what is probably the earliest and most significant characterization of the God of Israel—namely, the warrior. Consistently throughout the psalms, God is referred to as the "LORD of hosts" (Psalms 24:10; 46:8, 12; 58:9; 59:6; 69:7; 80:5, 8, 15, 20; 84:2, 4, 9, 13; 89:9). The Hebrew word צפאות (*sabaoth*) is a military term meaning "armies." The reference might be to celestial armies, meaning companies of minor deities or angels. It could also be to political forces, referring to squadrons of fighting personnel. This idea raises a very interesting connection with ancient Near Eastern creation narratives. In several of those traditions, creation occurs at the end of a cosmic battle between the forces of good and the forces of evil—evil often portrayed as a water monster. In these stories, creation unfolds as the effect of a mandate of the victorious god of order, with each celestial being assigned a place in the heavens. A palace is then constructed in the highest heaven from which the conquering cosmic hero rules over heaven and earth.

Several of these creation themes are found in psalms:

LORD, God of hosts, who is like you?
    Mighty LORD, your faithfulness surrounds you.
You rule the raging sea;
    you still its swelling waves.

You crush Rahab with a mortal blow;
with your strong arm you scatter your foes.   (Psalm 89:9–11)

By the LORD's word the heavens were made;
by the breath of his mouth all their host.   (Psalm 33:6)

The LORD has set his throne in heaven;
his dominion extends over all.   (Psalm 103:19)

Who is like the LORD our God,
enthroned on high,
looking down on heaven and earth?   (Psalm 113:5–6)

To you I raise my eyes,
to you enthroned in heaven.   (Psalm 123:1)

Israel's experience of deliverance from bondage in Egypt is brought together with ancient creation theology here in the psalms, producing new and creative thinking. The God of Israel who delivered the people from Egyptian servitude is really the cosmic warrior who at the time of creation defeated the forces of evil. Thus, we see the close relationship between the themes of deliverance and creation.

Ancient Israel believed that since God delivered all of creation from the power of cosmic evil, and since this same God rescued the people from the shackles of Egyptian bondage, God would certainly hear the cries of the downtrodden and the poor at any other time and rescue them from their misery. This explains the great number of laments found in the collection of the psalms. There are individual cries for help (Psalms 3–7, 13, 38–40, 51, 88, and so forth) in which the petitioner cries for release from harassment or from some illness, and there are communal laments (Psalms 14, 58, 80, 94, 126) that arise from national humiliation or distress. While these prayers express both grief and complaint, they usually also contain sentiments of confidence based on remembrance of past deliverance. This assurance of divine assistance is also prominent in psalms of confidence, both individual (Psalms 11, 16, 91, 131) and communal (Psalms 15, 125, 129).

Integrity of Creation

Although "integrity of creation" is a contemporary expression, the reality to which it refers was held in high regard by the ancient Near Eastern world, and it continues to be prized by most traditional societies today. The phrase "integrity of creation" was defined by the World Council of Churches at a consultation (held at Annecy, France) in 1988 as: "The value of all creatures in and for themselves, for one another, and for God, and their interconnectedness in a diverse whole that has unique value for God." This perspective is attentive to the intrinsic value of all creatures, not merely for their instrumental value to human concerns, as is the case with a more anthropocentric (human-centered) point of view, but in and for themselves. Respect for the intrinsic value of creation is clearly evident in several of the psalms, where God is praised for the wonders of the natural world and, on occasion, nature itself is invited to praise God.

Other ancient Near Eastern nations may have associated the process of natural creation with a cosmic battle between forces of good and forces of evil, but ancient Israel eventually came to see that there could not have been such a battle, for there was only one God, and all the natural forces of the cosmos were creatures of that God. The sun, the moon, and the stars were neither major nor minor deities, as many other ancient Near Eastern religious traditions claimed. Instead, these heavenly bodies came from the hand of this God:

> [Y]ou set the moon and sun in place.   (Psalm 74:16)

> . . . the moon and stars that you set in place.   (Psalm 8:4)

Psalm 104 lists some of the awe-inspiring marvels that God brought forth in the beginning and continues to sustain in the heavens (verses 2–4) and on earth (verses 5–23). The waters that other nations perceived as chaotic monsters were channeled into water courses by this divine creator (verses 6–9, 25–26). The ancient Israelites maintained that the God who delivered them from Egyptian oppression was actually the "maker of heaven and earth" (Psalms 16:15; 121:2; 124:8; 134:3; 146:6).

The psalmists were rhapsodic in their reflections of these wonders of creation:

> The heavens declare the glory of God;
>> the firmament proclaims the works of his hands.
>>> (Psalm 19:2)

Simply by being what they were created to be, they reveal the power and majesty, the creativity and beauty of God. Not only has God made this world magnificent, but also fecund and nurturing:

> You visit the earth and water it,
>> make it abundantly fertile.   (Psalm 65:10; also verses 11–14)

In many psalms, the natural world is personified, expressing delight in the natural order established by the creator:

> Let the heavens be glad and the earth rejoice;
>> let the sea and what fills it resound;
>> let the plains be joyful and all that is in them.
> Then let all the trees of the forest rejoice
>> before the LORD who comes,
>> who comes to govern the earth,
> To govern the world with justice
>> and the peoples with faithfulness.   (Psalm 96:11–13)

Perhaps the most remarkable personification of nature is found in Psalm 148, a psalm belonging to the collection known as Hallelujah Psalms (Hallelujah means "Praise the LORD"), because they begin and end with that traditional acclamation. In this psalm, all creatures are invited to praise the LORD. The sun, moon, and stars, considered deities in other ancient cultures, are here seen as creatures of God (verses 1–6). The heights of the heavens is the place of greatest honor; the hosts are military units of angelic defenders; the waters above the heavens are part of the original chaotic flood that was quelled by God and then assigned its place above the firmament. Every aspect of the heavenly realm was created by God and continues under God's control. They are all called upon to sing praise to the LORD.

The creatures of the earth are next summoned to praise God (verses 7–13). This includes the sea monsters and the ocean depths, which were considered by some to be chaotic forces; storm elements were revered as minor deities, agents of the mighty storm god. These natural marvels are all called to praise the creator along with the wonders of the earth, the animals that live on it, and the fruits that it produces. All are invited to praise the name of the LORD. Finally, the people of Israel are called to praise their God (verse 14). The psalm ends as it began: "Hallelujah!"

The Law and Wisdom

Closely associated with the theme of election is that of the importance of the Law. Respect for and observance of that Law was the primary way the people expressed their election by God. Many of the directives found in Israelite Law are simply social customs and practices drawn from the wisdom that emerged from life experience. Thus the Law and wisdom are very closely associated. While they often cover the same themes, they express these themes in significantly different ways. Wisdom offers counsel and advice, which can be freely followed or dismissed. The Law, on the other hand, states regulations and prohibitions and specifies sanctions for non-compliance. Furthermore, wisdom is usually expressed in generalities, while Law is quite specific. For example, a wise saying asserts:

A foolish son is vexation to his father,
and bitter sorrow to her who bore him. (Proverbs 17:25)

However, the Law states:

Honor your father and your mother, that you may have a long life in the land the Lord your God is giving you. (Exodus 20:12)

Though at times the Law might appear to be burdensome, ideally it was considered a set of instructions that directed the people on a path toward God. This positive attitude toward the Law is found in several psalms. One example is Psalm 19, where the Law is described as "refreshing the soul," "rejoicing the heart," and "enlightening the eye" (verses 8, 9). It is deemed "more desirable than gold . . . sweeter also than honey" (verse 11). Psalm 119 is a remarkable song of praise to the Law. Each of its 176 verses applauds some aspect of the Law. It is considered "my delight" (verse 24) and a source of hope (verses 49 and 81); it is the subject of study (verse 97), a light for the path (verse 105), and the measure for judging what is right (verse 164). This psalm claims that the worthiness of the Law flows not from its enlightened character or social acceptability, but from the righteousness of God:

> You are righteous, LORD,
>> and just are your judgments.
> You have given your testimonies in righteousness
>> and in surpassing faithfulness.　　　(Psalm 119:137–138)

It is clear that the Law was cherished and the people believed that it set them apart as God's special people.

Fidelity to the Law and failure to observe it also provided an explanation for the good fortune the Israelites enjoyed or the hardships that they had to endure. This ethical guide, which states that goodness is rewarded and evil is punished (known as retribution), served as an explanation of situations in which the people found themselves. It was also an incentive for obedience and a deterrence for unfaithfulness. Many psalms, whether hymns, laments, affirmations of wisdom, prayers of confidence or thanksgiving, express some facet of this theory of retribution:

> Many are the sorrows of the wicked one,
>> but mercy surrounds the one who trusts in the LORD.
>>> (Psalm 32:10 — thanksgiving)

> The wicked plot against the righteous
>> and gnash their teeth at them.
>>> (Psalm 37:12 — wisdom psalm)

> The LORD withholds no good thing
>> from those who walk without reproach.
>>> (Psalm 84:12 — song of Zion)

The LORD watches over all who love him,
  but all the wicked he destroys

(Psalm 145:20 — hymn)

As important as this theory of retribution might have been to the Israelites, they were convinced that punishment would not have the final word. If they would but acknowledge their culpability and return to God, they would be lavished with divine mercy:

For day and night your hand was heavy upon me;
  my strength withered as in dry summer heat.
Then I declared my sin to you;
  my guilt I did not hide.
I said, "I confess my transgression to the LORD,"
  and you took away the guilt of my sin.   (Psalm 32:4–5)

Have mercy on me, God, in accord with your merciful love;
  in your abundant compassion blot out my transgressions.
Thoroughly wash away my guilt;
  and from my sin cleanse me.
For I know my transgressions;
  my sin is always before me.   (Psalm 51:3–5)

The themes of retribution and mercy are interwoven throughout the psalms of lament, confidence, and thanksgiving, providing a theological framework for those religious feelings.

While the Law was considered to be revealed by God and specific to Israel, wisdom had universal value. It grew out of life experience common to all people. It was the fruit of reflection on the consequences of this experience, not divine ordinance, that determined whether an action was appropriate or not. Wisdom thinking claimed that wise behavior engendered happiness, while foolish behavior brought misfortune. While this pattern appears to be a form of retribution, it is really an example of the relation between act and consequence. The reward or punishment associated with Law was administered from an agent outside the action; however, in wisdom writing, happiness or misfortune flow directly from the action itself. In other words, these consequences were built right into the experience of life.

Ancient Israel believed that there were three facets to wisdom. The first was the general wisdom that could be gleaned from reflection on life experience:

> The just walk in integrity;
>> happy are their children after them! (Proverbs 20:7)

In addition to this experiential wisdom, the sages taught that true wisdom was found in commitment to the God of Israel, thus adding a religious dimension to it:

> The beginning of wisdom is fear of the LORD,
>> and knowledge of the Holy One is understanding.
>>> (Proverbs 9:10)

Finally, they maintained that not even religious fidelity could grasp the ultimate dimension of wisdom. This kind of wisdom belonged to God alone. It was personified as a woman and she resided with God:

> The LORD begot me, the beginning of his works,
>> the forerunner of his deeds of long ago. (Proverbs 8:22)

The wisdom psalms are more like instructions than they are prayers. However, they are instructions that teach by inference. They describe a situation in life to encourage one to pursue behavior that results in happiness or to avoid behavior that brings sorrow. Psalm 1 is a perfect example of this kind of teaching:

> Blessed is the man who does not walk
>> in the counsel of the wicked,
> Nor stand in the way of sinners,
>> nor sit in company with scoffers.
> Rather, the law of the LORD is his joy;
>> and on his law he meditates day and night.
> He is like a tree
>> planted near streams of water,

that yields its fruit in season;
    Its leaves never wither;
    whatever he does prospers.

But not so are the wicked, not so!
    They are like chaff driven by the wind.
Therefore the wicked will not arise at the judgment,
    nor will sinners in the assembly of the just.
Because the LORD knows the way of the just,
    but the way of the wicked leads to ruin.

The wise or righteous person is fruitful and life-giving, while the foolish or wicked person is worthless. It is clear which scenario is desirable, but the choice is up to the individual. It is often difficult to distinguish wisdom teaching from the requirements of Law because the language from these two traditions is often interchanged:

Those who do evil will be cut off,
    but those who wait for the LORD will inherit the earth.
                (Psalm 37:9 — considered to be a wisdom psalm)

It is important to remember that in ancient Israelite thinking, good Law originates from reflection on life experience. In other words, Law should be grounded in wisdom.

CHAPTER 3

The Liturgy: Privileged Setting for the Word of God

The Mass: Psalms in the Lectionary

> Sacred Scripture is of the greatest importance in the celebration of the liturgy. For it is from Scripture that the readings are given and explained in the homily and that psalms are sung."
> *Constitution on the Sacred Liturgy (Sacrosanctum Concilium)* (SC), 24

This passage from the first document issued by the Second Vatican Council, on December 4, 1963, highlights the significance of Scripture in the celebration of liturgy. It was because of this insight on the vital role of Scripture in the liturgy that the Council Fathers, in the same document, mandated that a far greater variety of Scripture be proclaimed in the liturgy than had been before the Council:

> The treasures of the Bible are to be opened up more lavishly, so that a richer share in God's word may be provided for the faithful. In this way a more representative portion of holy Scripture will be read to the people in the course of a prescribed number of years. (SC, 51)

Pope Benedict's apostolic exhortation *Verbum Domini* builds on this notion, asserting that the liturgy is the privileged setting for the Word of God (52). Indeed, he writes, "every liturgical action is by its very nature steeped in Sacred Scripture." These three statements show that Scripture is important for liturgy, and liturgy is important for Scripture. This relationship is particularly significant because the celebration of the Eucharist is the primary, and for many believers the only, setting in which they engage with the Word of God.

This chapter is concerned with the role the psalms play in the liturgy. It addresses the issues found in part 2 of *Verbum Domini*, entitled "Verbum in Ecclesia", or "The Word in the life of the Church." To appreciate those insights, we must first recognize the place of the Responsorial Psalm in the ritual. Although the readings and the psalm we hear at Mass have been taken from the Bible, a new literary context is created when they are brought together in the Lectionary and assigned to be proclaimed on specific days in the liturgical year. The Roman Catholic Church is a lectionary-based Church. That means that we read lections (lessons or readings) that are excerpts of a biblical passage. These passages are collected in the Lectionary, a book arranged according to the liturgical year. We do not read from a pulpit Bible itself, but from the Lectionary. Often verses from the original biblical text are omitted so that the desired theological focus of the text can be emphasized during the liturgical celebration. When people feel the need to restore these omitted verses so that the passage mirrors the original biblical passage, they misconstrue the purpose of a lectionary.

After the Council, the greater role for Scripture and the increased number of readings required a new lectionary with a new organization — for Sundays and for weekdays. Sunday Masses would now have three readings plus the psalm response (as opposed to only two readings in the lectionary before the Council), and instead of providing choices for only one liturgical year, three years of Sunday readings would now be provided, each drawing on the Gospel account of a different synoptic evangelist (Matthew, Mark, and Luke). Thus in our current Lectionary, Year A draws from Matthew, Year B from Mark, and Year C from Luke. The Gospel according to John appears on most of the Sundays of Easter, for Holy Thursday, for the Passion on Good Friday, and in Year A on the Third, Fourth, and Fifth Sundays of Lent (intended to accompany the scrutinies in the Rite of Christian Initiation of Adults). John also appears in the latter part of Year B, completing the liturgical year after the very short Gospel according to Mark ends. Readings for weekdays are provided for two years, labeled Year I and Year II.

The Lectionary, with its careful selection and grouping of passages, all arranged in a deliberate order, creates a liturgical context from which we are to interpret the psalms. However, even this new context changes, depending upon the day or liturgical time or season being celebrated. On memorials, feasts, or solemnities, the theology of that observance sets a theological character for the interpretation of the readings and psalm response. This is also the case during the liturgical seasons of Advent, Christmas Time, Lent, Triduum, and Easter Time. Since no specific theological themes are identified during Ordinary Time of the liturgical year, there is no particular theological context within which the readings and the psalm response should be interpreted. However, the Gospel readings during Ordinary Time sketch the life and ministry of Jesus, and the First Readings recount examples of ancient Israelites responding to God's action in their lives. Thus one might say that discipleship is a prominent theme — accounts of followers of God in ancient Israel and the example of Jesus for those who would be his disciples during his lifetime and today.

The Lectionary creates a liturgical context from which we are to interpret the psalms.

Finally, the organization of the Lectionary is an important literary matter, even as it serves a theological purpose. This chapter will discuss the organization and both the literary and the theological roles played by the Responsorial Psalms. Since the concern here is psalms in the liturgical life of the Church, we will be looking at the "world in front of the text," the world of the contemporary believer. However, historical information (the world behind the text) will be provided when necessary to throw light on the meaning of the passage under consideration.

Just what is liturgy, and why is it so important? The *Catechism of the Catholic Church* (CCC) explains the meaning of the word *liturgy*.

Originally it meant "a 'public work' or a 'service in the name of/on behalf of the people.' In Christian tradition it means the participation of the People of God in 'the work of God'" (CCC, 1069). Thus liturgy is a public event, consisting of both word and action. While the word and action components are most clearly defined in the Sacrament of the Eucharist as Liturgy of the Word and Liturgy of the Eucharist, both word and action components are found in other sacraments as well. The sacramental actions differ according to the specific sacrament, however the words employed in their celebration are always drawn from Scripture. The preceding sketch of the liturgical significance of Scripture enables us to better appreciate the explicit role played by the Responsorial Psalm. A careful look at various Responsorial Psalms will throw light on their importance in the liturgy. The *General Instruction of the Roman Missal* issued by the Congregation for Divine Worship and the Discipline of the Sacraments (2010) describes the position and importance of the psalm in the order of readings:

> After the First Reading follows the Responsorial Psalm, which is an integral part of the Liturgy of the Word and which has great liturgical and pastoral importance, since it fosters meditation on the Word of God. (61)

It also underscores the essential role of the psalm and all Scripture in the liturgy:

> Nor is it lawful to replace the readings and Responsorial Psalm, which contain the Word of God, with other, non-biblical texts.[1] (57)

If, as *Verbum Domini* points out, Scripture functions as a human response to divine self-revelation, this is explicitly the case during the liturgy, where the Responsorial Psalm focuses the assembly's response on a specific theme articulated in the First Reading. A look at the structure of the Liturgy of the Word and the way its readings are chosen will clarify this.

In all Liturgies of the Word, the Gospel passage is considered the principal reading. During Ordinary Time, Gospel passages follow a semicontinuous format, meaning that the Gospel reading for one Mass begins where the Gospel reading for the previous Mass ended. Although Sunday Masses and weekday Masses are on different cycles, this is the case for both. On weekdays, the First Readings, like the Gospel passages, follow a semicontinuous format. This practice has been adopted so that in the course of a year the Christian community attending weekday Mass will have reflected on the major points of one or several biblical books.

For the Sundays of Ordinary Time a different principle operates for the First Reading; in fact the method of choosing Sunday

---

1. Compare with John Paul II, apostolic letter, *Vicesimus quintus annus* (December 4, 1988), 13 in *Acta Apostolicae Sedis* 81 (1989): 910.

readings is slightly different from that of weekdays. On Sundays there are three readings, and there appears to be no thematic connection between the First and Second Readings. Whereas both the Sunday Gospel passages and Second Readings follow a semicontinuous pattern, the First Reading is selected because it shares a theme or themes with the Gospel passage. The Responsorial Psalm (both on Sundays and weekdays), is usually chosen because it highlights a theme or themes contained in the First Reading. This means that on Sundays there is often a thematic link between the Gospel passage, the First Reading, and the psalm verses that respond to the First Reading. Such a theme or themes should be considered the primary, though not exclusive, theological theme of that Sunday.

Another important factor is the theological significance of the solemnity being celebrated. It determines the choice of the three readings. Since the First Reading always governs the choice of the psalm, one might say that the theological significance of the solemnity governs the choice of readings and psalm response. Examples will make this dynamic clear.

How the Responsorial Psalm Interacts with the Other Readings

Monday of the Second Week of the Year, Year I

(This day of the liturgical year falls in January, immediately after the close of Christmas Time.) While both the First Reading and the Gospel passage follow their respective semicontinuous pattern, the psalm passage is a response to the First Reading. In the Gospel passage (Mark 2:18–22), Jesus teaches that the things in the past— signified by the fasting of John the Baptist and the Pharisees— must be left behind, and the new things—signified by Jesus—must be embraced. The First Reading (Hebrews 5:1–10) acclaims the royal priesthood of Christ:

You are my Son:
this day I have begotten you;
just as he says in another place,
You are a priest forever
according to the order of Melchizedek.

(Hebrews 5:5–6)

The psalm response is taken from a royal or Davidic Psalm:

"Yours is princely power from the day of your birth,
in holy splendor;
before the daystar, like dew, I have begotten you."
The LORD has sworn, and will not repent:
"You are a priest forever according to the order
of Melchizedek." (Psalm 110:3–4)

Being begotten by God is a royal theme; mention of Melchizedek is a priestly theme. In the context of this Christian celebration, the two themes combine and highlight the royal priesthood of Christ. The royal priesthood theme appears in both the First Reading and the Responsorial Psalm. Although the Gospel foregrounds Christ as something new that cannot be understood in terms of old practices, there is no connection to the theme of his royal priesthood in the Gospel passage.

Wednesday of the Sixteenth Week of the Year, Year II

The Gospel passage (Matthew 13:1–9) recounts a parable of Jesus in which he tells of a farmer who sows seed. The seed falls on ground of various quality. This passage furthers the semicontinuous reading of the Gospel found in previous and following days. The First Reading (Jeremiah 1:1, 4–10) begins the semicontinuous reading of the message of the prophet Jeremiah. In it, God assures the reluctant Jeremiah that God will be with him as he assumes the responsibilities of his prophetic call. In fact, God claims to have chosen Jeremiah even in his mother's womb. The psalm response (Psalm 71:1–6, 15, 17) might well have been recited by Jeremiah. In it, the psalmist turns to God for strength and protection, even claiming:

from my mother's womb you are my strength. (verse 6)

Here we see vividly the relationship between the First Reading and the psalm response.

Twenty-Third Sunday of Ordinary Time, Year B

The Gospel reading from Mark recounts the healing of a man who was deaf (Mark 7:31–37), an event that takes place on the Decapolis, a league of ten Gentile cities in the Transjordan (the land east of the Jordan River). That Jesus heals the man is not unusual, but that he does it outside the land of Israel is. The poetic First Reading, from the prophet Isaiah, looks into the future (Isaiah 35:4–7a), describing what will occur at the time of messianic fulfilment:

> Then will the eyes of the blind be opened,
> the ears of the deaf be cleared. (verse 5)

The people believed that at the time of fulfillment, all suffering and pain will cease and people will enjoy freedom and peace. The psalm response (Psalm 146:7–10), a hymn praising God for being gracious to the vulnerable, addresses some of these messianic characteristics:

> [the Lord]
> secures justice for the oppressed,
> gives food to the hungry.
> The Lord sets captives free.
>
> The Lord gives sight to the blind;
> the Lord raises up those who are bowed down. (Psalm 146:7–8)

The Second Reading, which is taken from the Letter to James, warns against showing more respect to the wealthy than to the poor (James 2:1–5). As important as this admonition is, it does not carry forward the theme of messianic fulfillment.

The passage from Isaiah is prophetic, looking toward messianic fulfillment; the psalm response lists aspects of divine providence; the Gospel passage presents Jesus' healing action as evidence of the inbreaking of the long-awaited messianic fulfillment accomplished through the graciousness of divine providence. The relationship between the First Reading and the Gospel passage is one of promise and fulfillment. However, the theme of messianic fulfillment does not end there. The Gospel introduces another theme: inclusivity. Jesus' healing was not limited to the Jewish people, nor was it reserved for those in the circle of people who followed him. The healing took place in Gentile territory, in the land of the outsider. The Gospel appears to expand the theme of the First Reading and Responsorial Psalm by suggesting that the joys and blessings of messianic fulfillment are open to all.

Thirty-Fourth Sunday in Ordinary Time, (Our Lord Jesus Christ, King of the Universe) Year A

The Gospel reading from Matthew (Matthew 25:31–46) depicts the Last Judgment as a time when all the nations will appear before the Son of Man. Appearing in the guise of a shepherd, he will separate the sheep (the righteous) from the goats (the wicked) and mete out the appropriate judgment. It is this description of the Son of Man as shepherd that determines the choice of the First Reading, a passage from the prophet Ezekiel (Ezekiel 34:11–12, 15–17). There God is characterized as a shepherd, but this picture differs from the portrayal of the shepherd found in the Gospel passage. Ezekiel's shepherd painstakingly gathers the scattered flock, providently brings them to rich pastures, and tenderly cares for the sick and the injured. Finally, the figure of the shepherd found in the Responsorial Psalm (23:1–3, 5–6) mirrors the characterization of God found in this First Reading more than the one in the Gospel passage. Rather than further the theme of shepherd, the Second Reading (1 Corinthians 15:20–26, 28) discusses the benefits that believers enjoy from the Resurrection of Christ.

Two rather different profiles of the shepherd appear.

It is clear that the shepherd theme is prominent on this Sunday, however two rather different profiles of the shepherd appear.

Although the readings do not really interpret each other, the two profiles of shepherd sit side by side and each influences our interpretation of the other. The Gospel reading determines the theme, and the descriptions found in the First Reading and the Responsorial Psalm refine that profile. The shepherd in the Gospel passage who judges does so in the gentle and caring spirit described in the First Reading and the Responsorial Psalm.

Commemoration of All the Faithful Departed (All Souls' Day)

A Responsorial Psalm can generate more than one liturgical response. This is evident in the way Psalm 23, which is the Responsorial Psalm for Our Lord Jesus Christ, King of the Universe, also functions in the liturgy for All Souls' Day. There one of the Gospel readings appointed for the celebration (John 6:37–40) speaks of Jesus raising up individuals on the last day. The First Reading recommended to be paired with that Gospel, from the Book of Wisdom (Wisdom 3:1–9) is a well-known passage that places the souls of the righteous in the hands of God, safe from the torments of death and destruction. Psalm 23 is often chosen as a response because of one specific verse:

> Even though I walk in the dark valley
>   I fear no evil; for you are at my side
> with your rod and your staff
>   that give me courage.   (Psalm 23:4)

Since All Souls' Day is a special commemoration, all three readings and the psalm passage are recommended because they reflect some aspect of the observance itself. This explains the choice of the Second Reading (Romans 6:3–9), where we find Paul speaking of the power of the Resurrection of Christ Jesus that raises those believers who have died. All of the readings speak of death. The First Reading and the psalm response assure the believer that those who die continue to enjoy the tender care of God, even in the face of death. The Gospel passage and the Second Reading assure them that this divine graciousness comes to us through the Resurrection of Christ.

Feast of the Exaltation of the Holy Cross

Crucifixion was an ancient Roman method of capital punishment. The naked victim was tied or nailed to a beam that was then affixed to the top of a pole. The entire weight of the body was then supported by the out-stretched arms. This frequently caused the dislocation of shoulder and elbow joints. When this happened, or when the victim was overcome by this strain, the body simply collapsed, breathing became impossible, and the victim died of asphyxiation. After the crucifixion of Jesus, the Christian community gradually transformed the horror and disgrace of his ordeal into an exaltation of the holy Cross.

The Christian community gradually transformed the horror and disgrace of Jesus' ordeal into an exaltation of the holy Cross.

The religious meaning of this feast influenced the selection of readings chosen for its celebration. The Gospel passage recounts the exchange between Jesus and Nicodemus (John 3:13–17). Trying to explain what it means to be born again, Jesus recalls an episode from the story of Moses, and this very episode is described in the First Reading (Numbers 21:4b–9). Despite God's care for them in the wilderness, the people complained. As punishment for their faithlessness, God sent desert serpents to bite and sicken them. God then instructed Moses to make an image of a serpent, and whoever looked upon this image was healed:

> Moses accordingly made a bronze serpent and mounted it on a pole, and whenever anyone who had been bitten by a serpent looked at the bronze serpent, he live. (Numbers 21:9)

The bronze serpent that was actually a sign of their sin and of God's judgment became the means of their deliverance. Jesus says that, as was the case with the people and the serpent, those who believe in him when he is lifted up will have eternal life:

And just as Moses lifted up the serpent in the desert, so must the Son of Man be lifted up, so that everyone who believes in him may have eternal life. (John 3:14–15)

The psalm response is taken from Psalm 78, a sketch of God's involvement in the history of Israel from the time of the earliest ancestors to the time of David. Although there is no explicit mention of the bronze serpent here (Psalm 78:1–2, 34–38), the text describes both God's punishment for their sin and their eventual forgiveness. In the Second Reading (Philippians 2:6–11) we find an explicit reference to Christ's cross — his reprehensible death by crucifixion in verse 8, and his ultimate exaltation (verses 9–10). Thus these three readings explicitly and the psalm response implicitly testify that the ignominious instrument of Jesus' misery and disgrace has been transformed into the glorious means of our salvation and an offer of eternal life.

Second Sunday of Advent, Year A

Scripture must be interpreted within its particular context. For example, a passage that praises the king might have originally had David in mind. However, when it is read during Christmas Time, it refers to Jesus, the new-born king; when it appears at the end of Lent or during Holy Week, it calls to mind the man of sorrows who was crowned with thorns. Responsorial Psalms are meant to be interpreted in this way.

Contrary to what many might think, the liturgical readings for Advent seldom refer to the upcoming birth of Jesus. Rather, they call us to ponder God's restoration of a broken people. Sometimes God is perceived as restoring this people directly, at other times restoration is seen as occurring through the agency of a great leader — a king, a priest, or a prophet. In the Gospel passage for this Advent Sunday (Matthew 3:1–12), John the Baptist announces that this restoration, referred to as the Kingdom of Heaven, is at hand. Turning to the First Reading (Isaiah 11:1–10), the prophet speaks about this restoration and the one who will bring it to pass. He speaks of it as being in the future. In the Gospel passage, Jesus speaks of it as being at hand. The psalm response (Psalm 72:1–2, 7–8, 12–13, 17) reflects the description of peace and fulfillment described in the Isaiah passage. However, because the context is the season of Advent, the meaning of the readings and the psalm response moves away from Isaiah's Israel and John's desert to the season of Advent in our own day. As we reflect on our own brokenness and how we long for someone to lead us to a time and place of fulfillment, Isaiah's idyllic scene of peace and justice becomes our dream, and the king's son mentioned in the psalm (Psalm 72:2) becomes the one of whom John speaks (Matthew 3:11). Even the reading from Paul (Romans 15:4–9) becomes personal when we hear:

> Whatever was written previously was written for our instruction, that by endurance and by the encouragement of the Scriptures we might have hope. (Romans 15:4)

Were such insights and sentiments intended by the original biblical authors and psalmists? Probably not, but then they were addressing people of their own times who were facing their own challenges. Principles that govern reading from the perspective of the "world in front of the text" remind us that sometimes words spoken or written by one person are comprehended by another in a very different way.

The Epiphany of the Lord

Verses from Psalm 72 serve as the Responsorial Psalm for the Epiphany of the Lord as well. But because of the specific religious meaning of this solemnity (the manifestation to the world of the divinity and glory of Christ), the Responsorial Psalm emphasizes different theological themes. The Gospel reading is the account of the visit of the Magi, first to the court of Herod in Jerusalem and then to the place where the child was found in Bethlehem (Matthew 2:1–12). While the prophetic passage that comprises the First Reading (Isaiah 60:1–6) was originally a message of hope for the inhabitants of the beleaguered city of Jerusalem, the passage is replete with details that lend themselves to an Epiphany interpretation. For example:

> Rise up in splendor, Jerusalem! Your light has come,
>> the glory of the Lord shines upon you.   (verse 1)
>
> Nations shall walk by your light,
>> and kings by your shining radiance.   (verse 3)
>
> Caravans of camels shall fill you,
>> dromedaries from Midian and Ephah;
>
> All from Sheba shall come
>> bearing gold and frankincense,
>> and proclaiming the praises of the Lord.   (verse 6)

In addition to the reference to the king's son already mentioned above, two verses of the psalm that were omitted in the Advent response are included here:

> The kings of Tarshish and the islands shall offer gifts;
>> the kings of Arabia and Seba shall bring tribute.
>
> All kings shall pay him homage,
>> all nations shall serve him.   (Psalm 72:10–11)

These are simply two examples of how the season in which the psalm is read can add a dimension of meaning to the psalm response and other readings.

Psalms and Liturgical Music

Finally, a word should be said about the way liturgical music relates to Scripture, especially to the psalms. After the Second Vatican Council, contemporary composers responded deliberately to the emphasis on Scripture in the *Constitution on the Sacred Liturgy* and began composing songs with far more Scripture either quoted or paraphrased than had been available earlier. Thus, there is much to choose from today.

It is not enough to choose hymns the congregation might know. Ideally, hymns should relate to the day's Scripture readings as the Responsorial Psalm does, by somehow expressing the theme or themes contained in the readings and enhancing that message. Besides psalm responses that have been set to music, many contemporary liturgical hymns are interpretations or expansions of psalmic themes.

For example, the lyrics of the hymn "Center of My Life"[2] follow almost exactly the words of Psalm 16, which is an individual psalm of confidence. Only the refrain is a new composition that reinforces personal faith. The hymn "Glory and Praise to Our God,"[3] without repeating the wording of Psalms 65 and 66, was inspired by them. Psalm 65 is a communal hymn of thanksgiving, while Psalm 66 is a composite prayer. The refrain praises both natural creation and God's protection in the events of history.

Hymns should relate to the day's Scripture readings as the Responsorial Psalm does.

Two very different hymns have been inspired by Psalm 91, an individual prayer of confidence. "On Eagle's Wings"[4] follows very closely the words of several verses of the psalm; the refrain is original. In "Blest be the Lord,"[5] most of the lyrics are a paraphrase of the words of the psalm, with a change from second person descriptive ("You shall not fear . . .") to first person declarative ("I shall not fear . . .").

Psalm 98, a hymn of praise, is the inspiration of "Sing a New Song."[6] Although this song contains some of the language and certainly the ideas in the psalm, the lyrics do not follow the psalm's text closely. In "O God, You Search Me," Bernadette Farrell has done a very close paraphrase of Psalm 139, set to a melody that captures the intimacy of the prayer.[7] John Michael Talbot's composition "Come, Worship the Lord" is based on Psalm 95, and "Only in God" is based

2. Paul Inwood, refrain "Center of My Life" (OCP Publications, 1985).

3. Daniel L. Schutte, "Glory and Praise to Our God" (OCP Publications, 1976).

4. Michael Joncas, "On Eagle's Wings" (New Dawn Music, OCP Publications, 1979).

5. Daniel L. Schutte, "Blest be the Lord" (New Dawn Music, OCP Publications, 1976).

6. Daniel L. Schutte, "Sing a New Song" (OCP Publications, 1972, 1974, 1979).

7. Bernadette Farrell, "O God, You Search Me" (OCP Publications, 1992).

on Psalm 62.[8] Christopher Walker has closely followed the words of Psalm 27 in "The Lord Is My Light" and Marty Haugen's "Sing Praise to God" follows Psalm 146.[9]

It is clear from these reflections that the theme and religious feelings found in the Liturgy of the Word of any particular liturgical celebration are not happenstance. Insightful liturgical preparation will allow the themes of the readings and the Responsorial Psalm to be enhanced by the careful selection of appropriate music. Ideally, all of this is then made explicit in the unfolding of the homily.

---

8. For both of these: John Michael Talbot (Birdwing Music/Cherry Lane Music, 1980).

9. Christopher Walker, "The Lord Is My Light" (OCP Publications, 1996); Marty Haugen, "Sing Praise to God" (GIA Publications, Inc., 2009).

CHAPTER 4

How Ritual Elements of the Mass Enrich Our Experience of the Psalms[1]

Liturgy's Framework for the Word of God

The Mass has a stately structure and unhurried character that invites participants to notice and absorb the meaning of its words and actions. Many of those words come from Scripture, and many of the liturgical actions of the Mass draw our attention to those words of Scripture, helping us recognize in them the presence of the Lord.

For example, in the Introductory Rites, the words of the entrance chant are often taken from a psalm (GIRM, 48) — usually a psalm of praise and thanksgiving. In the entrance procession, the Book of the Gospels is carried through the midst of the assembly and placed on the altar, helping the assembly recognize that, as the General Instruction of the Roman Missal puts it (28), the Liturgy of the Word and the Liturgy of the Eucharist are "so closely interconnected that they form but one single act of worship."[2] With our own eyes we see the Word presiding at the table of the Lord.

The Liturgy of the Word has its own framework — a structure of seven parts, four for each of the four proclamations, followed by the homily, profession of faith, and the intercessions or universal prayer. We will focus on the first four parts — the readings. Each

---

1. This chapter was contributed by the editor, Lorie Simmons.

2. Cf. SC 56; Sacred Congregation of Rites, instruction, *Eucharisticum mysterium* (May 25, 1967), 3: Acta Apostolicae Sedis 59 (1967): 542.

Scripture proclamation is framed by ritual words, gestures, actions, and pauses for silence — an important element according to the General Instruction of the Roman Missal:

> The Liturgy of the Word is to be celebrated in such a way as to favor meditation, and so any kind of haste such as hinders recollection is clearly to be avoided. In the course of it, brief periods of silence are also appropriate, accommodated to the assembled congregation; by means of these, under the action of the Holy Spirit, the Word of God may be grasped by the heart. (56)

It can be helpful to review the way the readings unfold within their four-part framework, noting how the ritual words, gestures, actions, and pauses help the assembly attend to the Scripture — and especially how they facilitate the role of the psalm. Part 1 begins as the reader of the First Reading walks with dignity to the ambo, the privileged place for proclaiming Scripture. A ritual statement introduces the reading: "A reading from the book of . . ."; for example, "A reading from the book of the prophet Isaiah." The reader proclaims "in a loud and clear voice" in a way appropriate to the text of the reading itself (GIRM, 38). The manner and tone of the reader is important because "When the Sacred Scriptures are read in the

Church, God himself speaks to his people, and Christ, present in his word, proclaims the Gospel" (GIRM, 29). The reader closes the reading by pausing and then initiating an acclamation: "The word of the Lord" and the assembly responds "Thanks be to God." The reader returns to a designated seat and a brief silent pause follows. Part 1 has concluded.

Part 2 begins when the psalmist approaches the ambo to lead the Responsorial Psalm. She or he sings the refrain and then gestures by lifting one or both hands for the assembly to repeat the sung refrain. The psalmist then sings the verses, gesturing for the assembly to sing the refrain at intervals. As the people become more familiar with the melody of the refrain, the unified voice of the assembly becomes stronger until by the last repetition of the refrain the people are usually singing with comfort and heartfelt conviction. When the assembly has sung the last refrain, the psalmist pauses briefly and returns to her or his usual place. The second part of the Liturgy of the Word has concluded.

After another brief silent pause, the reader of the Second Reading walks to the ambo and repeats the pattern of the First Reading. Since the Second Reading is often taken from one of the New Testament epistles or letters, the assembly now hears the voice of a Christian teacher speaking directly to a congregation, and often it is a bracing message. The second reader departs from the ambo. The third part has concluded.

The fourth part, the high point of the Liturgy of the Word, begins when the second reader has departed from the ambo, after another pause. Special marks of honor accompany the reading of the Gospel. Through these, "the faithful acknowledge and confess that Christ is present and is speaking to them" (GIRM, 60). To begin with, all stand. If there is a deacon, he goes to the celebrant to receive a blessing. The cantor alone or the choir sings the Alleluia (or in Lent, the verse before the Gospel), and the assembly joins in. The deacon (or celebrant) moves to the altar, takes the Book of the Gospels, and processes to the ambo, flanked by altar servers bearing lit candles.

Once at the ambo, he introduces the reading with an acclamation "A reading from the Gospel according to . . . ," simultaneously tracing a small cross on the book, then on his forehead, lips, and heart. The people respond with the words "Glory to you, O Lord" as they sign themselves with a small cross on their forehead, lips, and heart. If it is a solemn occasion, the Gospel reader may incense the Book of the Gospels. The reading ends with the closing acclamation, "The Gospel of the Lord," and the assembly responds, "Praise to you, Lord Jesus Christ." The people are seated and the fourth part of the Liturgy of the Word concludes.

All of these framing words, gestures, movements, and pauses slow the pace of our thoughts and draw attention to the words within the frames. In this structure, the Responsorial Psalm stands out as the poetic selection of Scripture that is sung by the assembly. We take the words of the refrain—which express a key theme of the day's Scripture readings—into our own mouths and send them out as a prayer to God. The words and melody remain in our consciousness, ready to continue our prayerful response to God at another moment.

Psalms in a Communal Celebration

Although the psalms speak powerfully to individuals in the midst of their personal situations, when assemblies sing the psalm response together during the liturgy, they, like their ancient Hebrew ancestors who sang in synagogue or Temple, are especially mindful of its meaning for the whole people of God. The people respond to God as a community. The memory of our moments of private prayer with those same psalms intertwines with our communal psalm-singing and the communal moments fortify our personal prayer. The conviction with which we sing the psalms in the assembly also fortifies each other.[3]

The people respond to God as a community.

---

3. The fourth-century saint from Alexandria, St. Athanasius, had a great devotion to the psalms. In a letter to Marcellinus (a man who had written to him, asking for advice on reading

Singing Psalms

Although the Responsorial Psalm may be recited rather than sung, the General Instruction of the Roman Missal makes it clear that singing is the preferred practice (GIRM, 61). In the liturgy, singing is the way we imbue a text with special meaning and solemnity.

During much of the Liturgy of the Word, the assembly is listening. This is not a passive role, for the people listen attentively, meditating on what they hear, making connections with the other readings, prayers, songs, and actions of the liturgy. With the Responsorial Psalm, the rhythm of the liturgy changes, and the assembly is called to an even more active role. Now the congregation sings the refrain together.

The responsorial structure for psalm-singing, now so familiar to western Catholic assemblies, was developed by Joseph Gelineau during the 1950s as an alternative to Gregorian chant. This method allowed the congregation to sing the carefully crafted refrain and so interact more closely with the words and meaning of the psalm. Fr. Gelineau's other contribution to psalm-singing was a translation from Hebrew (first in

Together we follow the melody. Together we breathe.

French and later in English) of the psalter. His translation is admired for respecting the rhythms of the original language. That English translation, known as the Grail translation, has gone through subsequent revisions, the most recent by the monks of Conception Abbey in Missouri, and is now authorized for use in the liturgy in the United States.

---

the psalms), Athanasius explains that "Within [the Psalter] are represented and portrayed in all their great variety the movements of the human soul. It is like a picture, in which you see yourself portrayed, and seeing, may understand and consequently form yourself upon the pattern given. . . . It seems to me, moreover, that because the Psalms thus serve him who sings them as a mirror, wherein he sees himself and his own soul, he cannot help but render them in such a manner that their words go home with equal force to those who hear him sing, and stir them also to a like reaction" (*Letter to Marcellinus*, 11, 12).

The music for Responsorial Psalms is composed to express the attitude that words of the psalm convey, so that singing the melody of the refrain takes us more deeply into the words. Singing also yokes us to a group action — to each other. Together we follow the melody. Together we breathe. Together we give voice to the theological theme expressed in the psalm refrain that highlights an insight in the First Reading or Gospel. The refrain is repeated several times, and with each repetition, the words of the psalm, expressed in melody, penetrate more deeply into our consciousness. Days later the refrain can return to mind, allowing assembly members to pray with a key theological theme of the previous Sunday during their week.

The Lectionary provides the option for parishes to use a seasonal Responsorial Psalm rather than the psalm for the day. In that case an assembly comes to know the psalm very well, taking in the words week after week. During the course of the season, the refrain and many phrases from the psalm will enter into the people's memories.

The Psalms as Sacred Scripture

Although set to music, the words of the Responsorial Psalm we sing are clearly Scripture, and not a modern poetic composition. To emphasize that the psalm, too, is Sacred Scripture, some parishes ask the psalmist or cantor to lead the singing of the psalm from the ambo — the privileged place for the proclamation of Scripture in the liturgy.

CHAPTER 5

The Psalms and
the Sacraments

S ome of the sacraments are celebrated within the context of the Eucharist. As a result, believers might not always recognize the ways that the specific rites for these sacraments give the Mass a special significance that differs from a weekday or Sunday Mass. This is certainly true with regard to Ordination, Confirmation, and Marriage, as well as adult Baptism, which takes place on Holy Saturday as part of the Sacred Triduum. Sacraments celebrated in a Eucharist include a Liturgy of the Word similar to that found in the other celebrations of the Eucharist. However, just as the theologies of the high liturgical seasons (Advent, Christmas Time, Lent, Triduum, and Easter Time) influence the choice of readings during those times, so the theology of the respective sacrament influences the choice of the readings, including the Responsorial Psalm. A closer look at the rites of infant Baptism, Matrimony, and Anointing of the Sick will illustrate this. These sacraments have been chosen because they are probably the ones most frequently experienced by the average believer.

Infant Baptism

The *Rite of Baptism for Children* begins with greetings extended to the child to be baptized, the parents, and the sponsors, followed by a preliminary series of questions about the reasons that prompted the desire for Baptism. If the rite is celebrated at a regular Sunday Mass, the readings for that Sunday are used. However, if it is a Sunday in Christmas or Ordinary Time, the readings may be taken from the section of the Lectionary for the conferral of infant Baptism (756–760) or from those included in the rite itself. One or more passages are to be read, and between the readings Responsorial Psalms may be sung. While it is up to the celebrant and the parents to decide which of the recommended readings will be used, several of them, with suggested Responsorial Psalms, will be discussed here.

Various readings from both the Old and the New Testaments are provided in the ritual book. Old Testament passages include the accounts of the water from the rock (Exodus 17:3–7), the promise of clean water (Ezekiel 36:24–28), and water coming from the Temple (Ezekiel 47:1–9, 12). Readings from New Testament letters include reflections on sharing in Christ's death and Resurrection through Baptism (Romans 6:3–5), justification though Christ (Romans 8:28–32), being baptized in one Spirit (1 Corinthians 12:12–13), being baptized into Christ (Galatians 3:26–28), one Baptism in Christ (Ephesians 4:1–6), and being a chosen race (1 Peter 2:4–5, 9–10). Twelve Gospel passages are provided. Those that specifically relate to Baptism are accounts of Jesus sending his disciples to baptize (Matthew 28:18–20), the baptism of Jesus (Mark 1:9–11), Jesus' discussion of new birth with Nicodemus (John 3:1–6), his discussion of water with the Samaritan woman (John 4:5–14), and his teaching on thirst for living water (John 7:37b–39a).

A glance at these readings reveals the importance of water. Water, like other sacramental symbols, always has more than one meaning. Contrary to the understanding of many, it is not the

Water, like other sacramental symbols, always has more than one meaning.

cleansing property of water that is most emphasized by the rite, but its saving and refreshing quality and its chaotic, threatening character. Both the *Catechism of the Catholic Church* and the general introduction *Christian Initiation* emphasize that the primary aspect of baptismal water is its ability to join us to the Lord's death and Resurrection and to the Church: "The 'plunge' into the water symbolizes the catechumen's burial into Christ's death, from which he rises up by

Resurrection with him as 'a new creature'"[1] and "Baptism incorporates us into Christ and forms us into God's people."[2] (Obviously this dynamic is at work in the Baptism of an infant just as it is in the Baptism of an adult catechumen.) Another meaning of baptismal water, given more emphasis in other times, is that it "washes away every stain of sin, original and personal, makes us sharers in God's own life, and his adopted children."[3] It is the primary understanding of water, as found in the theology of the sacrament, that is most clearly stated in the readings taken from Paul's writings. Again and again he speaks of being baptized into Christ's death and rising into the new life gained through Christ's Resurrection. Being plunged into water ritually enacts the sense of being swallowed up by the forces of death; rising out of water signifies being born into new life. Those movements reflect the ancient mythological conflict between the forces of evil and death (characterized as chaotic waters), and the forces of good and life (reflected in life-giving water), resulting in victory.

The second understanding of water found in the readings points to its ability to refresh this new life. From this focus comes the idea of living water. Baptismal water always raises issues of life and death, rather than merely cleansing. The human experience of water always poses a paradox. On the one hand, it represents what is chaotic and threatening; on the other hand, it is life-giving and refreshing.

Three psalms are suggested as responses: Psalm 23:1b–3a, 3b–4, 5, 6; Psalm 27:1bcde, 4, 8b–9abe, 13–14; and Psalm 34:2–3, 6–7, 8–9, 14–15, 16–17, 18–19. While the choice of the readings will guide the choice of psalms, certain concepts within the psalm passages lend themselves to baptismal themes. "Beside restful waters he leads me;" and "he refreshes my soul" (Psalm 23:2) certainly suggest new and peaceful life after evil and the threat of death have been conquered.

---

1. Regarding "new creature," compare Council of Florence (DS, 1314): *vitae spiritualis ianua*. Quotation from CCC, 1213.

2. *Christian Initiation*, General Introduction, 2.

3. See 2 Peter 1:4; *Christian Inititiation*, General Introduction, 5.

"One thing I ask of the LORD / . . . To dwell in the house of the LORD / all the days of my life" (Psalm 27:4) expresses the soul's desire to belong to the new community, the people of God. "The angel of the Lord encamps / around those who fear him, and he delivers them" (Psalm 34:8) refers to deliverance from the threat of death. As discussed above, the context in which a psalm is sung focuses that psalm's theological connection with the particular liturgical celebration. Ideally, the assembly's appreciation of these themes of water, belonging, and deliverance would be enhanced by the homily.

The refrains of these psalms also express baptismal themes. "The Lord is my shepherd, there is nothing I shall want" expresses trust in the soul's new life in the shepherd's flock. The refrains "The Lord is my life and my salvation," "Wake up and rise from death" (both for Psalm 27), and "Look to him that you may be radiant with joy!" (Psalm 34) all allude to the saving light of Christ they will soon receive in the form of their baptismal candle, lit from the Paschal candle. "Taste and see the goodness of the Lord" seems to suggest the Eucharist that will eventually bring the initiates into full communion with their Lord and the Christian community.

The way these psalm responses emphasize the water theme throws light on the blessing of the water that soon follows in the baptismal ritual. This blessing echoes many of the water images found in the readings: the Spirit breathing over the chaotic waters at the time of creation; rescue from the chaotic waters of the flood; safe passage through the chaotic waters of the Red Sea; Jesus' baptism in the waters of the Jordan; the saving water that flowed from his pierced side; and the admonition to baptize with water "In the name of the Father, and of the Son, and of the Holy Spirit." This focus on water enables participants to appreciate the fundamental meaning of Baptism. Obviously the infant will be helped to make these

The web of meanings arising from the readings, prayers, and ritual actions of this rite will enrich the parents, who will be the primary catechists of the child.

connections later in life. The expressive and intricate web of meanings arising from the readings, prayers, and ritual actions of this rite will enrich the parents, who will be the primary catechists of the child, as well as the assembly gathered to celebrate and welcome the new Christian into the life of the community.

Matrimony

The Liturgy of the Word for the Sacrament of Matrimony usually consists of three readings. As is the case with all celebrations of the Liturgy of the Word, the First Reading is from the Old Testament and is followed by the Responsorial Psalm. All of the passages listed in the ritual focus on some aspect of the theology of the sacrament.

Old Testament readings include passages from: the creation narratives, where the first couple is told to increase and multiply (Genesis 1:26–28, 31), and where the man and the woman are said to be suitable partners for each other (Genesis 2:18–24). There are also accounts of the marriages of Jacob and Leah and Jacob and Rachel as well as Tobiah and Sarah (Genesis 24:48–51, 58–67; Tobit 7:6–14; Tobit 8:4b–8). A wisdom reading (Proverbs 31:10–13, 19–20, 30–31) describes the woman of worth, prompting many current-day readers to receive it as a meditation on the qualities of an ideal spouse, whether female or male. There is love poetry in the Song of Songs (Song of Songs 2:8–10, 14, 16a; 8:6–7a), a description of the fruits of a happy marriage (Sirach 26:1–4, 13–16), and an account of the covenant made between God and the people (Jeremiah 31:31–32a, 33–34a). These readings clearly highlight various aspects of human love and commitment. The liturgical context of matrimony obviously prompts us to interpret these readings in the light of marriage. The readings from the New Testament letters (not all of which are mentioned here) place that love within the context of Christ's love for us (Romans 8:31–35, 37–39; 1 John 3:18–24; Revelation 19:1, 5–9a) and Christian love of others (Romans 12:1–2, 9–18; 1 Corinthians 12:31–13:8a; Colossians 3:12–17; 1 John 4:7–12). They insist on respect for one's body (1 Corinthians

6:13c–15a,17–20), and they admonish mutual love and respect between husband and wife (Ephesians 5:2a, 21–33; 1 Peter 3:1–9). Some people might find these two passages troubling because they reflect gender-biased patriarchal customs of the day.

The psalm responses are either hymns praising God for blessing (Psalm 33:12 and 18, 20–21, 22; Psalm 103:1–2, 8 and 13, 17–18a; Psalm 145:8–9, 10 and 15,17–18; Psalm 148:1–2, 3–4, 9–10, 11–13a, 13c–14a) or wisdom psalms that describe the happiness that comes from living a good life: (Psalm 34:2–3, 4–5, 6–7, 8–9; Psalm 112:1bc–2, 3–4, 5–7a, 7bc–8, 9; Psalm 128:1–2, 3, 4–5ac and 6a). As mentioned so many times in this book, while the feelings expressed in the psalms are rather general, the context in which they are sung adds a degree of specificity to their meaning. Thus, the blessings for which God is praised are perceived as the blessings of human love and marriage; the happiness described flows from the bond of love that exists between the woman and the man. The refrains of these psalms distill their key themes, such as "The earth is full of the goodness of the LORD" and "Blessed are those who fear the Lord."

Only two of the suggested Gospel passages provide explicit teaching on marriage itself (Matthew 19:3–6 and Mark 10:6–9). The others offer Jesus' teaching for ways of living that will bring forth the reign of God, the goal of any and every Christian life. These readings include passages from the Sermon on the Mount (Matthew 5:1–12a; 5:13–16; and 7:21, 24–29). There are also passages containing Jesus' teaching about love of God (John 15:9–12; 15:12–16; and 17:20–26) and love of others (Matthew 22:35–40). Finally, Jesus' participation in the celebration of the wedding feast at Cana (John 2:1–11) shows his delight in the celebration of marital love enjoyed by the newly married couple and their guests.

The readings and psalm responses do not simply encourage human love. They presume that such love is already present. The readings situate that human love within the context of divine love,

The refrains of these psalms distill their key themes.

characterizing it as an expression of divine love that is empowering. They encourage mutual fidelity, especially through difficult times. They also remind the couple that they are not alone in their love; they are part of a community with whom they are now responsible in a new way to bring forth and nurture the reign of God. This is all the more explicit when the assembly gathered for the wedding Mass sings the refrain of the Responsorial Psalm, expressing their support of the couple and their faith that Christ will be present and active in their marriage.

Anointing of the Sick

Pope Benedict's document *Verbum Domini* contains a very strong statement about the power of the Word of God when used in the Sacrament of the Anointing of the Sick:

> In the case of the sacrament of the Anointing of the Sick too, it must not be forgotten that "the healing power of the word of God is a constant call to the listener's personal conversion."[4] (VD, 61)

The rite envisions two situations for the recipient of this sacrament—one in which someone is suffering from an illness or some form of physical infirmity from which that person might or might not recover, and the second circumstance in which death is imminent. While the format of the Liturgy of the Word and the principles employed in selecting readings and psalm responses are similar on both occasions, the passages themselves are often significantly different. The theme in the first instance is trust in God for healing; the theme of the second is trust in God in the face of death. In both instances, the ritual begins with an appropriate greeting, which may be followed by a sprinkling of holy water, a reminder of Baptism. After this comes the penitential rite and then the Liturgy of the Word.

---

4. This passage from *Verbum Domini* (61) quotes from the first paragraph of *Propositio*, the document containing recommendations of the Twelfth Ordinary General Assembly of the Synod of Bishops, The Word of God in the Life and Mission of the Church, which met in 2008.

Readings from the Old Testament for the Anointing of the Sick are taken from the First Book of Kings (19:4–8), from Job (3:3,11–17, 20–13; 7:1–4, 6–11; 7:12–21), from the Book of Wisdom (9:1a, 9–18), and from Isaiah (35:1–10; 52:13–53:12; 61:1–3a). All these readings have themes of suffering and illness, trust in God, or strength and healing. The same themes are found in New Testament readings taken from the Acts of the Apostles (3:1–10; 3:11–16; 4:8–12; 13:32–39), and various letters of Paul (Romans 8:14–17; 8:18–27; 8: 31b–35, 37-39; 12:1–2; 1 Corinthians 1:18–25; 12:12–22, 24b–27; 15:1–4; 2 Corinthians 4:16–18; Galatians 4:12–19; Philippians 2:25–30; Colossians 1:22–29). Passages from other biblical letters are also suggested (Hebrews 4:14–16, 5:7–9; James 5:13–16; 1 Peter 1:3–9; 1 John 3:1–2). One reading from Revelation is included (21:1–7).

One of the suggested psalm responses is the prayer of a suffering person taken from Isaiah (38:10–12, 16). The rest of the responses come from various psalms. Psalm 6:2–6, 9–10; Psalm 102:2–3, 24–28, 19–21; and Psalm 143:1–2, 5–6, 10 belong to a collection known as the Penitential Psalms. They express both repentance and confidence in God's mercy. Psalm 25:4–10,14–16; Psalm 42:1–3, 5; Psalm 43:3–5; Psalm 63:2–9; Psalm 71:1–2, 5–6, 8–9,14–15; Psalm 86:1–6, 11–13, 15–16; Psalm 90:2–6, 9–10, 12, 14, 16; and Psalm 123:1–2 are prayers of lament. While laments are psalms of complaint or cries for help, they often contain attitudes of confidence and thanksgiving. The psalmist may be overwhelmed by illness, the attack of enemies, or the threat of death, but the prayer is directed to God—evidence of confidence in God's concern and desire to rescue the one suffering. At times this confidence leads to profound gratitude. Still, these prayers of lament should be used with great caution, lest the theology of retribution (suffering as punishment for sin) become the primary focus of the celebration of the sacrament, rather than confidence in God's love even in the face of illness and suffering. This confidence is clearly seen in Psalm 27:1, 4–5, 7–10 and Psalm 34:2–7, 10–13, 6, 19. Finally, in Psalm 103:4, 11–18, the psalmist praises God for having heard the cries for help and shown compassion. The refrains of these recommended Responsorial Psalms encapsulate the themes mentioned already — repentance and confidence: "Have mercy on me, Lord, my strength is gone" (6), "To you, O Lord, I lift my soul" (25), "Put your hope in the Lord; take courage and be strong" (27), "My soul is thirsting for you, O Lord my God" (63), "In every age, O Lord, you have been our refuge" (90), and thanksgiving: "O bless the Lord, my soul!" (103).

The Gospel passages suggested for this sacrament are too numerous to list. Most of them are Gospel accounts of Jesus' healings; others contain lessons of encouragement. Those planning the celebration of the sacrament should choose readings that might in some way be linked with the condition of the one receiving the sacrament. The readings chosen should clearly emphasize God's concern for bodily and spiritual well-being.

Although the Anointing of the Sick is often administered privately, many parishes celebrate this sacrament periodically at a Sunday Mass. In that setting the Responsorial Psalm especially takes on a communal aspect. The refrain, sung by the entire congregation, affirms and fortifies the sick with the faith and prayer of the community.

The refrain, sung by the entire congregation, affirms and fortifies the sick with the faith and prayer of the community.

The readings for the Liturgy of the Word are significantly different when the suffering person is facing imminent death. In this case the setting for the sacrament is most likely private. Only two readings from the Old Testament are suggested for Viaticum. One is the account of Elijah who, when facing death received food and drink that enabled him to walk to the mountain of God (1 Kings 19:4–8). Analogously, the one dying is strengthened as she or he moves toward the eternal dwelling place of God. The second passage is from Job (19:23–27a), in which Job cries out: "I know that my vindicator lives, / and . . . I will see God." The readings from Paul (1 Corinthians 10:16–17 and 11:23–26) focus on the bread and wine of Eucharist, which in this situation becomes Viaticum. (In ancient Rome viaticum referred to provisions for travel.) The readings from Revelation (3:14b, 20–22 and 22:17:20–21) speak of the eschatological coming of Christ.

The Responsorial Psalms highlight the themes of confidence in God's loving care (Psalms 23:1–3, 4, 5, 6 and 145:10 and 14, 15–16, 17–18), God's deliverance of the one in need (Psalm 34:2–3, 4–5, 6–7, 10–11), longing for the presence of God (Psalm 42:2, 3, 5cdef; 43:3, 4, 5), and God's care for those who have died (Psalm 116:12–13, 15 and 16bc, 17–18). Any one of these passages would be an appropriate response to the story of Elijah's undertaking, Job's plight, or the eschatological messages found in Revelation. Either Psalm 23 or Psalm 145 would be a fitting response to the Eucharistic themes found in Paul's letters to the Corinthians because they both speak of believers being fed by God, resurrection of believers, and their eternal happiness with God. Here again, knowledge of the person who is facing death should influence the choice of readings and response. Some people will need to be assured of God's mercy and forgiveness; others will be able to rest quietly, confident that they are already united with God. Readings for Viaticum should relieve anxiety and enable one to die in peace.

CHAPTER 6

The Psalms in Liturgies of the Word Outside of Mass

Non-Eucharistic Liturgies of the Word would include funerals outside of Mass, communion services, distribution of ashes, visits to the sick, and miscellaneous prayer services. In most of these cases, an important component of the service is a Liturgy of the Word, consisting of appropriate biblical passages with a psalm response.

There are really three different steps in the funeral liturgy: the vigil or wake service, the funeral itself, and the committal to the ground. According to the directives issued by the United States Conference of Catholic Bishops, the vigil service can take the form of a Liturgy of the Word accompanied by reflection and prayers. It can also take the form of one of the prayers of the Office for the Dead from the *Liturgy of the Hours*. In either case, the psalms will constitute a significant portion of the service. Most likely, psalms of confidence will be most fitting here. Though it is a rather informal service, the vigil is a time to remember the life of the deceased and to commend her or him to God's mercy

The Gospel passage chosen determines the choice of the First Reading, which influences the choice of the psalm response.

and loving care. At this time we also ask God to console us in our grief and give us strength to support one another. Whether or not the funeral itself is part of the Eucharistic celebration, it includes a Liturgy of the Word containing psalms of confidence.

The rite for Holy Communion Outside Mass opens with a greeting followed by a penitential rite and then the Liturgy of the Word.

For these services the readings used may be those assigned to the liturgy of that day, readings from votive Masses for the Blessed Sacrament, or any reading that would be appropriate for that day. As is always the case, the Gospel passage chosen determines the choice of the First Reading, which influences the choice of the psalm response. Intercessions precede the actual reception of Communion, and concluding prayers bring the service to an end.

The blessing and distribution of ashes may also take place outside Mass. In this case, the readings for the Liturgy of the Word are those assigned to the Mass for Ash Wednesday: Joel 2:12–18; Psalm 51:3–6ab, 12–14, and 17; 2 Corinthians 5:20–6:2; and Matthew 6:1–6,16–18. The reading from the Gospel teaches about the importance of the three major penitential practices: prayer, fasting, and almsgiving. The First Reading, from the prophet Joel, picks up the theme of fasting; the psalm response prays for mercy; the Second Reading reminds us that we have been reconciled with God through Christ. These are the themes that call believers into the season of Lent.

The occasion of the visit and the choice of reading determine the choice of the psalm response.

The rite for visits to the sick that do not include the Sacrament of Anointing consists of a reading with a psalm response, the Lord's Prayer, concluding prayers, and a blessing. While the choice of reading might be suggested, none is assigned. As is always the case, the occasion of the visit and the choice of reading determine the choice of the psalm response.

CHAPTER 7

The Psalms in the Liturgy of the Hours

In Contrast to the Liturgy of the Word— Praying Psalms in Their Own Right

Divine Office, Liturgy of the Hours, and *Breviary* all refer to the same set of prayers. The expression *Divine Office* signifies an office or duty performed for God. *Liturgy* originally meant a public work or service in the name of or on behalf of the people. *Liturgy of the Hours,* then, refers to a public service that is performed at stated hours of the day. *Breviary* comes from the name of the book, which contains the prayers selected to be recited at those stated hours. The Second Vatican Council's document, *Constitution on the Sacred Liturgy (Sacrosanctum Concilium)* (SC) refers to this form of prayer as *Divine Office*; both *Verbum Domini* and the *Catechism of the Catholic Church* prefer the title *Liturgy of the Hours.* This latter designation will be used here, because it lends itself to the character of the discussion that follows.

Psalms function very differently when they are prayed outside of the celebration of any of the sacraments. There, in the Liturgy of the Word, which is a part of the sacramental ritual, they act as a prayerful response to lectionary readings. In the Liturgy of the Hours, they are prayers in their own right. Here, the religious sentiments they contain are themselves the focus of the prayer. When part of the Liturgy of the Word, only those verses that call attention to the theological theme that is the focus of the Gospel passage and the first reading are included in the psalm response. In the Liturgy of the Hours, the entire psalm is prayed. The Liturgy of the Hours does not follow the order of Psalms as found in the Psalter. Rather, the day is divided into various liturgical hours, and psalms are chosen for the respective hours that express various aspects of that time of day.

According to ancient Greek and Roman custom, the night and day were divided into four parts, each consisting of three hours. References to these divisions of the day can be found in various New Testament passages. There we read that Jesus tells a parable (Matthew 20:1–16) of a landowner who hired workers at dawn (verse 2), at the third hour (verse 3), at the sixth and ninth hours (verse 5), and at the eleventh hour (verse 6). Some contemporary Bibles translate these hours as 9:00 AM, noon, 3:00 PM and 5:00 PM). Jesus is said to have been crucified at the sixth hour (Matthew 27:46; Mark 15:25); and, on the day of Pentecost, the Holy Spirit descended upon the Apostles at the third hour (Acts 2:15).

There is biblical evidence of a correspondence between this division of the day's twenty-four hours and the custom of praying several times a day. Though the psalms do not state particular hours when prayer should be offered, they do speak of times of the day in general:

> I cry out to you, Lord;
> > in the morning my prayer comes before you.   (Psalm 88:14)

> At midnight I rise to praise you
> > because of your righteous judgments.   (Psalm 119:62)

> Seven times a day I praise you
> > because your judgments are righteous.   (Psalm 119:164)

These passages show that praying at certain times of the day was a long-standing tradition. The hours of the day are specific in New Testament writings:

Peter went up to the roof terrace to pray at about noontime [sixth hour]. (Acts 10:9)

Now Peter and John were going up to the temple area for the three o'clock hour [ninth hour] of prayer. (Acts 3:1)

About midnight, while Paul and Silas were praying and singing hymns to God . . . (Acts 16:25)

The practice of praying at certain times of the day is very common in many cultures that foster religious devotion. The most basic of such prayers includes prayer at the beginning of the day and prayer just before retiring at night. To this practice Christians added the Angelus, which consisted of reflections on the mysteries of the life of Jesus. Times for this prayer were signaled by the ringing of church bells at six in the morning, at noon, and at six in the evening. The scene of peasants stopping their work and bowing in prayer in the field was memorialized by Jean-François Millet in his 1859 painting *The Angelus*. Jews are obliged to pray three times a day: in the morning, in the afternoon, and at nightfall. The five times of Muslim prayer are determined by the position of the sun: at morning twilight when light appears across the width of the sky just before dawn; at midday after the sun passes its zenith; in the afternoon when the shadow of an object is the same length as the object itself; at sunset; and at night. These three Abrahamic traditions consecrate the entire day to the praise of God in these prayerful ways.

In the Jewish tradition, the day began (and continues to begin) in the evening ("Evening came, and morning followed"—Genesis 1:5, 8, 13, 19, 23, 31), and so the first hour of prayer was Evening Prayer, known in the Liturgy of the Hours as Vespers. The other hours that make up the Liturgy of the Hours are Compline, or Night Prayer, Matins, or night Vigils, also called the Office of Readings, Lauds, or prayer at dawn, and Prime, Terce, Sext, and None, the shorter daytime prayers. The foundation of this form of prayer is psalmody (the singing of psalms), which is arranged within these hours in such a way that the entire Psalter of one hundred fifty psalms is recited within the period of four weeks. In the past, the ordained (bishops, priests, and deacons) and members of monastic communities were obliged to pray all of the hours every day. The reform of the Second Vatican Council revised these requirements. Monastic nuns and monks continue to pray all of the hours at the appointed times. The ordained still pray all of the hours (choosing one of the three daytime prayers) as much as possible at the appointed times, (GLOH, 29). For those in consecrated life who are not in monastic communities, only Morning Prayer (Lauds), Evening Prayer (Vespers), and one of the shorter hours are required. Furthermore, Prime has been suppressed. These revisions recognize the far-reaching changes that have taken place in the lives of apostolic ministers. They acknowledge that while monastic life is organized around these times of prayer, the ministerial life is not.

Benedict XVI's *Verbum Domini* holds the Liturgy of the Hours in highest regard:

> Among the forms of prayer which emphasize Sacred Scripture, the Liturgy of the Hours has an undoubted place. The Synod Fathers called it "a privileged form of hearing the word of God, inasmuch as it brings the faithful into contact with Scripture and the living Tradition of the Church."[1] (VD 62)

After the Eucharistic celebration, the Liturgy of the Hours is considered the official public prayer of the Church,[2] marking the hours of each day and sanctifying the day with prayer. It is a faithful response to the biblical injunction, "Pray without ceasing" (1 Thessalonians 5:17). The Church that prays that public prayer, says the General Instruction of the Liturgy of the Hours, includes both the living and the dead:

> When the Church offers praise to God in the liturgy of the hours, it unites itself with that hymn of praise sung throughout all ages in the halls of heaven. (GILOH 16)

The *Catechism of the Catholic Church* (CCC) describes how the different elements of the Liturgy of the Hours interact with the psalms to create such a deep prayer form :

---

1. *Propositio*, 19.

2. *Constitution on the Sacred Liturgy (Sacrasanctum Concilium)*, 98.

The hymns and litanies of the Liturgy of the Hours integrate the prayer of the psalms into the age of the [Christian] Church, expressing the symbolism of the time of day, the liturgical season, or the feast being celebrated. Moreover, the reading from the Word of God at each Hour (with the subsequent responses or troparia) and readings from the Fathers and spiritual masters at certain Hours, reveal more deeply the meaning of the mystery being celebrated, assist in understanding the psalms, and prepare for silent prayer. (CCC, 1177)

Each hour follows essentially the same pattern. There is always psalmody, a reading from Scripture, and finally a prayer of petition. While all of the hours have their part to play in the official prayer of the Church, two hours are prominent:

Lauds as morning prayer and vespers as evening prayer are the two hinges on which the daily office turns; hence they are to be considered as the chief hours and are to be celebrated as such. (SC, 89a)

The Role of the Psalms in Each of the Hours

The psalms function in various ways in the different hours. Matins, now called the Office of Readings, is also called Vigils, because it is prayed at the time of a nocturnal vigil. The order of psalms recited generally follows the order found in the Psalter from Psalm 1–108, except when the theology of the feast or season being celebrated determines the selection of psalms. The hour begins with the simple, traditional *versicle* ("Lord, open my lips," sung by the leader of prayer) and response, "And my mouth will proclaim your praise," which prepares us for all the liturgical hours of the day. This introduction is followed by an *invitatory*, or invitation to prayer, which consists of a responsorial recitation of either Psalms 24, 67, 95, or 100 (three prayers of praise and one of thanksgiving) with an antiphon (or refrain) interspersed between verses. A hymn is sung next, followed by three psalms. The primary focus of this hour is the readings, which are taken from Scripture or from the writings of revered spiritual authors.

Lauds, or Morning Prayer, opens with the invitatory if the Office of Readings is not prayed. Otherwise it begins with the simple invitatory petition and response: "God, come to my assistance." "Lord, make haste to help me." This is followed by an appropriate song and then psalmody, which consists of a psalm, a canticle from the Old Testament, and a second psalm. Next are a short reading and response, the Canticle of Zachary (Benedictus), intercessions, the Our Father, and a final prayer. The psalms chosen are more than suitable for morning prayer:

In the morning you will hear me;   (Psalm 5:4)

In the morning my prayer comes before you.   (Psalm 88:14)

Morning Prayer is intended to sanctify the day at its beginning and to remind us of the Resurrection, the dawning of that day that will not end.

The first psalm in Morning Prayer might be a petition or a lament. Such a prayer at the beginning of the day serves to remind us of our human needs. However, it is really the second psalm that sets the tone for the entire hour and, thus, for the day. It is either a hymn of praise or a prayer of thanksgiving, which, in this context might be considered praise. In the morning, when the sun has overcome the forces of darkness, it is only fitting to praise God, even in the face of human need. Such hymns of praise acknowledge the power of God in creation that brings forth a new day, and that power in our lives which enables us to face this day with all of its challenges and possibilities. The Old Testament canticle that is prayed between the psalms calls to mind God's power as it was revealed at some time in the history of ancient Israel. This serves to instill trust that, as God protected the ancient Israelites, so God will protect us. The canticle of Zachary (Benedictus) brings the ideas expressed in the psalms to conclusion in a song of praise.

In the morning, it is only fitting to praise God, even in the face of human need.

Terce, Sext, and None, the shorter hours, are recited as closely as possible to midmorning, midday, and midafternoon. They have been preserved in the official prayer of both the Eastern and Western Churches because they are reminders of the hours of Jesus' passion and death. Terce, the third hour after dawn, was also remembered as the time of Pentecost, when the Holy Spirit transformed the followers of Jesus into fearless disciples (Acts 2:15). Sext, the hour when the sun is at its highest, was the hour when Peter had his rooftop vision that prompted the early Church's acceptance of Gentiles into their number (Acts 10:9). None marks the hour when Jesus died (Matthew 27:46; Mark 15:34; Luke 23:44). These Hours begin with the invitatory verse and response, followed by the singing of an appropriate song, the recitation of three psalms or parts of psalms which are in some way connected with the respective time of day. An example of a fitting theme would be the importance of the Law in directing one's daily activity:

> The law of the Lord is perfect,
> it revives the soul.
> The rule of the Lord is to be trusted,
> it gives wisdom to the simple. (Psalm 19:8)

The shorter hours end with a short reading, and a concluding prayer.

Terce, Sext, and None are prayed during the ebb and flow of the day, the real span of time within which we live. Therefore, the focus of the psalms that constitute this prayer is the discovery and following of the way of righteous living. This explains why Psalm 119 is the basis of such prayer. This wisdom psalm of one hundred seventy-six verses acclaims the value and reliability of the Law for accomplishing this goal. The second and third psalms of these hours encourage this righteous living. Thus, these hours provide moments of pause during the day when we seek strength through prayer for the resolve we made in the morning.

Vespers, generally referred to as Evening Prayer, is the hour of the setting of the sun. It is a time to raise our minds, hearts, and hands in praise and thanksgiving:

Let my prayer arise before you like incense,
the raising of my hands like an evening oblation. (Psalm 141:2)

The structure of Evening Prayer is very similar to that of Morning Prayer: invitatory verse and response, appropriate song, psalmody consisting of a psalm, a canticle from the New Testament, a second psalm, a reading from Scripture with response, the Canticle of Mary (Magnificat), intercessions, the Our Father, and a final prayer. At the end of the day, the theme is fulfillment. Within the context of this hour of Christian prayer, the royal psalms that are used take on a Christological character. The canticle from the New Testament is also a hymn of praise to Christ. At evening, just as the day is on the threshold of its fulfillment, so do we come to see the fulfillment of God's promises of old. We join Mary in her Magnificat, which now becomes ours as well.

Vespers is the last official prayer of the day for those who only pray in the morning and in the evening. However, Compline, or Night Prayer, is really the final hour, ideally, prayed in darkness. Its simple format lends itself to memorization. It begins with the standard invitatory vesicle and response. An examination of conscience is optional. This is followed by an appropriate hymn, a psalm, a short reading from Scripture with response, the Canticle of Simeon (Nunc Dimittis), concluding prayer, and blessing. The hymns for Night Prayer are generally prayers of trust. The darkness and mystery of night foreshadow the darkness and mystery of death. Thus we turn to God and cry out: "Into your hands I commend my spirit" (Psalm 31:6). At the completion of Compline, one of the four Marian anthems is sung: Alma Redemptoris Mater (Loving Mother of Our Redeemer), sung during Advent and Christmas season; Ave Regina Caelorum (Hail, Queen of Heaven), sung during Lent; Regina Caeli (Queen of Heaven), sung during the Easter season; or Salve Regina (Hail, Holy Queen), sung outside of any liturgical season. Thus the Liturgy of the Hours ends with an anthem honoring Mary.

Sacrosanctum Concilium states:

> Christ Jesus, high priest of the new and eternal covenant, taking human nature, introduced into this earthly exile the hymn that is sung throughout all ages in the halls of heaven. He joins the entire human community to himself, associating it with his own singing of this canticle of divine praise.

> For he continues his priestly work through the agency of his Church, which is unceaselessly engaged in praising the Lord and interceding for the salvation of the whole world. The Church does this not only by celebrating the eucharist, but also in other ways, especially by praying the divine office. (SC, 83)

Thus, praying the psalms in the Liturgy of the Hours is a major way in which we participate in the priestly work of Christ. Even when the hours are prayed alone, it is not merely the individual who prays, but the Church that prays. Joined with Christ, the Church offers prayer to the all-holy God.

CHAPTER 8

Entering into the Psalms through Lectio Divina

An Ancient Practice

The wisdom and power of the psalms can be accessed in still other ways. People often turn to Scripture at significant moments in their lives, looking for guidance, encouragement, or support—seeking inspiration that might provide direction in life. Although such seekers might not realize it, when they turn to Scripture in such prayerful reflection, they are engaging in an abbreviated form of the age-old practice of *lectio divina* or "sacred reading."[1]

The practice of lectio divina is traced back to the third century when Origen began to explore the possibility of discovering a deeper meaning to Scripture than was immediately apparent in reading. He sought ways to allow the meaning of the passage to "touch" the listener or reader. Private reflection on Scripture was popular in Eastern monasticism in the fourth century and an essential part of monastic life and prayer in the West by the sixth century. Today this kind of prayer is generally associated with the Benedictines, for St. Benedict insisted that prayerful reflection on Scripture be a vital part of the lives of all his monks. In his apostolic exhortation *Verbum Domini*, Pope Benedict followed the lead of his patron when he stated that such prayer should be part of the spirituality of all members of the Church, not merely monks:

---

1. "Within [the Psalter] are represented and portrayed in all their great variety the movements of the human soul. It is like a picture, in which you see yourself portrayed, and seeing, may understand and consequently form yourself upon the pattern given" (St. Athanasius, *Letter to Marcellinus*, 11).

The Synod frequently insisted on the need for a prayerful approach to the sacred text as a fundamental element in the spiritual life of every believer, in the various ministries and states in life, with particular reference to *lectio divina*. (VD, 86)

This approach to reflective reading of Scripture brings to fulfillment various passages of the New Testament:

> "The word is near you,
>   in your mouth and in your heart." (Romans 10:8)

Indeed, the word of God is living and effective, sharper than any two-edged sword, penetrating even between soul and spirit, joints and marrow, and able to discern reflections and thoughts of the heart. (Hebrews 4:12)

Lectio divina should not be confused with the study of Scripture, which is a technical approach that seeks to uncover the meaning of the passage. Rather, lectio divina is an approach that seeks to immerse one in the spiritual meaning of the passage in order to shape or strengthen one's relationship with God. While there are various ways of engaging in lectio divina, the best-known method appeared in the twelfth century in a book entitled *The Ladder of Monks*, written by a Carthusian monk named Guigo. Employing the biblical image of Jacob's ladder (Genesis 28:12), Guigo envisioned this ladder as moving from earth to heaven. He identified four rungs in this mystical ladder: *lectio* or reading; *meditatio* or meditation; *oratio* or prayer; and *contemplatio* or contemplation. While these rungs or steps seem distinct from each other when the approach is analyzed, there is significant movement back and forth when one is engaged in the practice.

The four steps have sometimes been linked to the four levels of medieval biblical interpretation devised by John Cassian in the fifth century; namely, literal, allegorical, tropological, and anagogical. The literal meaning is the straightforward meaning of the passage; allegorical refers to the non-literal or hidden meaning of the passage; tropological is its moral sense; and anagogical signifies its meaning as pointing to the eschatological, future fulfilment of God's plan. A thirteenth-century poem captures these four approaches to interpretation:

> The literal sense teaches what happened,
> The allegorical teaches what to believe.
> The moral teaches how to act,
> The anagogical teaches where things are going.[2]

These medieval ways of explaining how to interpret Scripture are not essential to the practice of lectio divina. They simply show that there have always been various approaches to reading and understanding the Bible. Over the years, lectio divina itself has consisted of as few as three and as many as eight steps. The discussion that follows uses the traditional version of four steps identified by Guigo.

Describing *Lectio*

The first step in this prayerful approach is to read the biblical passage. At first glance, this could appear to be the easiest step, when in fact it might be quite difficult. This is because we often tend to read much later theological interpretations into the biblical passage. For example, the story of the sin of the first human couple as found in Genesis 3 is often referred to as "the fall." A careful reading will show that no fall took place. There certainly is sin, but there is no mention of a fall. An immediate argument might claim that the first couple fell from grace, but grace is not an ancient Israelite concept, and a fall from grace is a much later Christian notion (Galatians 5:4). "Fall from grace" is then an interpretation read into the story, not a textual statement found in it. There is a point in lectio divina when one moves away from the biblical text itself and interprets what its message might mean for this moment of prayer, but it is not part of this first step, which deals with what is actually in the passage, with what the text says and what it means.

---

2. This Latin verse was often quoted: "Lettera gesta docet, quid credas allegoria, moralis quid agas, quo tendas anagogia."

Just as we might read something into the biblical passage that is not there, we can also miss what is there. For example, we often speak of the covenant that God made with Noah after the flood (Genesis 9:9–17). In so reading, we overlook the fact that the covenant was not made with Noah alone, but "with your descendants after you" (verse 9). In fact the covenant was made with "every living creature" (verses 10, 12, 15, 16), not simply human beings. These two examples show that simple reading is not always simple. There are times when we read what we expect to find, not what is actually in the passage.

How then is one to read the biblical text? In lectio divina it is important to read the passage slowly and thoughtfully, perhaps two or three times. Questions will help in this careful reading. (Since our focus here is the use of psalms in lectio divina, the questions asked will be specific to reflecting on psalms.) First, identify the feelings that are expressed: praise? lament? confidence? gratitude? Then, be aware of the circumstances in life that seem to have called forth these feelings. There will usually be more than one expressed; it is important to be attentive to all of the feelings and attitudes. Next, since the psalms are poetry, it will be important to probe the meaning of the creative imagery and the poetic literary forms found there.

> It is important to read the passage slowly and thoughtfully, perhaps two or three times.

If any study takes place in lectio divina it happens in this step. Since the psalm originated in an ancient time and culture, it might be helpful to consult a commentary for insight into the meaning of something in the psalm that is culturally unfamiliar. If the period of prayer is short, this can be done ahead of time. This search for information should not be minimized, for the more one grasps and appreciates the meaning of the passage, the greater will one's prayer be enriched.

Describing *Meditatio*

This step of meditation moves one into personal reflection. Just as the first step sought to discover what the biblical passage says and means in itself, this step seeks to find what the passage says and means to the one praying. This kind of meditation is not meant to break open the religious meaning of the passage (that happens in the first step), but to allow that meaning to break open one's mind and heart. When studying Scripture, the biblical passage acts as a window through which one can discover religious meaning. In lectio divina, the passage is more like a mirror into which one looks in order to discover something about one's own self. This does not mean that one engages in personal introspection or psychological self-analysis. Here it is the religious meaning of the passage that does the probing, not the person. One might say that this kind of meditation moves beyond the original meaning of the passage by enabling one to discover personal meaning in it.

This kind of meditation allows the meaning of the passage to break open one's mind and heart.

Questions can be helpful in this step as well: Which religious feelings or attitudes expressed in the psalm are resonating with you right now? What in your life calls forth such feelings or attitudes? Might these feelings spring from your personal life? from a relationship with another person or social group? What might this passage be saying to you today about the situations in which you find yourself? Are you comforted by these new insights? challenged? Do you welcome them, or resist them? Why or why not?

Describing *Oratio*

Prayerful reflection or meditation on ways in which the message of the biblical passage encounters one's life naturally leads to prayer. Examining the passage and how the religious meaning of that passage encounters one's life can bring one to spontaneous response. Questions are out of place in this step. When meditation opens the mind and heart, the mind and heart are disposed to respond in prayer. This prayer will be some form of personal response to God who has spoken specifically to this person through the message of the passage. Since God is the primary author of Sacred Scripture, God speaks to the modern-day believer just as God spoke to the ancient believer. Depending on one's disposition, this response might be praise of God for the wonders that one has experienced in life, confidence that God will protect and provide for one in the future, gratitude for the divine graciousness with which one has been blessed, repentance for infidelity or foolishness, or some form of petition.

This prayer is not simply a well-known or an ordinary form of prayer. Rather, it flows from fervent reflection on the Word of God. It is personal prayer that springs directly from one's enlightened inner being, and it may even happen that this prayer will be more an experience of religious feeling than an actual formulation of words. However it is expressed, this prayer is a response to God that is appropriate to the insights gained by prayerful reflection on what the Word of God might be saying at this moment in the person's life.

This prayer flows from fervent reflection on the Word of God.

Describing *Contemplatio*

The final step in this approach is a prayerful resting in the presence of God, a quiet realization of one's existence with God in praise, confidence, gratitude, or repentance. There is a definite movement to the steps of lectio divina. Lectio begins with a biblical passage; meditatio makes a personal connection with something found within that passage; oratio moves away from the passage and concentrates on the religious response that springs from that connection; contemplatio is one's peaceful resting in that religious response.

This kind of peaceful resting is itself a blessing. It engenders a realization of the presence of God and it draws one deeper into that realization. This is not an intellectual exercise. There is no need for words, for explanations. It is the kind of being together experienced by people who have loved each other and shared life for a long time. It is an experience of presence born of profound knowing and loving.

Strictly speaking, this kind of quiet resting is not an activity. In fact, if we are to attain it, we must learn to refrain from trying to direct it. Instead, we must hand ourselves over to it. This kind of emptying of oneself is difficult for people who are usually in control of their lives. While the first three steps of lectio divina are all about serious activity—critical reading, thoughtful reflecting, and prayerful responding—this last step is about humble receptivity.

Trying Out the Steps

Perhaps the best way of describing lectio divina is to illustrate how this practice of prayer might unfold.

> The LORD is my shepherd;
>> there is nothing I lack.
> In green pastures he makes me lie down;
>> to still waters he leads me;
>> he restores my soul.
> He guides me along right paths
>> for the sake of his name.
>> Even though I walk through the valley
>>> of the shadow of death,
>> I will fear no evil, for you are with me;
>> your rod and your staff comfort me.
> You set a table before me
>> in front of my enemies;
> You anoint my head with oil;
>> my cup overflows.
> Indeed, goodness and mercy will pursue me
>> all the days of my life;
> I will dwell in the house of the LORD
>> for endless days.
>
> (Psalm 23)

Step 1: *Lectio*

What does the passage say and what does it mean? Psalm 23 is an individual's prayer of confidence. God is characterized in two different ways, as a shepherd and as the host of a sumptuous banquet. As a shepherd, God finds pasture for grazing and water to quench the thirst of the flock; God is concerned with the sheep that stray or are lost, and guards the flock from predators and dangers of any kind. This shepherd attends to both the physical needs of the sheep and to the soul, which is the individual's very life force (this is a better translation of the Hebrew word *nephesh* נפש than "soul"). God's guidance is more than provident; it is also moral. God leads along the paths of righteousness. Darkness, whether a reference to the darkest part of the terrain, to personal gloom, or to death itself, does not instill fear in the psalmist, for the presence of the LORD is reassuring.

The second image is of a host who prepares a lavish banquet for guests. The strict Near Eastern code of hospitality obliged hosts to provide the very best provisions for guests, even those who were enemies. The LORD spreads out such a banquet here. It affords not only nourishment, but also a public witness to God's high regard for the psalmist. In this psalm, all needs are met, all dangers are countered, fear is vanquished, and the psalmist lives secure in the presence of God.

Step 2: *Meditatio*

What does the passage say and what does it mean for you, at this point in your life? Here is where the one praying connects the feelings found in the psalm with some present experience in life. The psalm presumes that the individual is in a very vulnerable situation. This could be unemployment, devastating financial loss, crippling failure, serious illness, and so forth. For the sake of this discussion, a diagnosis of cancer will be the situation. Such a diagnosis will elicit shock, fear, and perhaps anger. One now reads the psalm through this lens.

The very first verse speaks of total confidence in God. This might not be one's initial reaction when stricken with this alarming disease, but it is the underlying attitude of the psalm, the attitude to which the one praying hopes to aspire.[3] The rest of the psalm gives reasons for confidence. Even in the face of cancer, whatever one needs is available. Green pastures imply rich life; still waters are tranquil—the opposite of chaotic or unruly water. The rod and the staff of a shepherd are meant to ward off anything or anyone who might endanger the sheep. They are symbols of protection. Even in the face of the possibility of death from this frightening disease, the idea of God's protection can be comforting.

The image of a lavish banquet highlights the limitless resources of God. It suggests that there is nothing God is not willing to offer the one praying. An overflowing cup of wine reinforces this image, and anointing the head with oil is a celebratory practice. All of this denotes abundant enjoyment of life. Finally, dwelling in God's house means living in the presence of God.

Both characterizations of God are meant to instill confidence in God. The underlying hope of one with cancer is, of course, healing. However, the attitude is confidence in God. That means that one trusts in God regardless of the medical outcome. All of the imagery of tranquility and abundance points to God's providential care, whether in healing or in continued illness. The psalm leads the one praying to appreciate that the ultimate security is living in the presence of God.

Step 3: *Oratio*

One's prayer springs from this very personal meditation. Crushing illness often challenges one's understanding of how life is supposed to unfold. When unexpected hardship of any kind thwarts one's plans, one might turn to God in anger, thinking that God is not being faithful

---

3. In one of his many sermons on the psalms that St. Augustine delivered in his cathedral at Hippo, he advised his congregation on how to enter into a psalm and receive its wisdom: "If the psalm prays, then you pray; if it grieves, then you grieve; if it exults, then you rejoice; if it hopes, then you hope; if it fears, then you fear" (Exposition 2, Psalm 30.3.1).

to the way God should act. This often results in a challenge of one's own images of God. The prayer that springs from this meditation could be a prayer to be led out of anger or despair. It could be a prayer for patience, strength, and acceptance. Whatever the prayer might be, it flows from the world of faith carried within the one praying.

Any prayer that stems from personal meditation on Psalm 23 will be grounded in trust in God. Trust will enable one to accept frightening illness without anger or despair because meditation shows that illness does not mean abandonment by God. One can be patient and strong and rely on God's power because this trust is rooted in God's care regardless of what happens. God is indeed a loving and caring shepherd, and devastating illness does not negate this. God is a gracious host whose magnanimity far exceeds our needs. This is the kind of prayer that might spring from one's personal reflection on the attitudes expressed in Psalm 23.

Step 4: *Contemplatio*

It is not possible to provide a detailed explanation of contemplation because it is not an activity under the control of the one praying. Ideally, it will be some kind of a resting in God in confidence. It might take the form of acceptance of one's illness; it could be a sense of security despite the possibility of death. Much depends upon the prayerful insights and religious needs of the one praying. Nor is it possible to decide how much time should be devoted to this step. It lasts as long as it will last. All one can do is engage in the process with honesty and openness, and leave the rest to God.

Many people today add a fifth step to the traditional four steps delineated by Guigo. That step is operatio or action. This fifth step moves the fruits of contemplation into action. It calls for some form of human response to the insights gained and the prayerful resting in God experienced. This could be a concrete action, or it could be an inner strengthening in one's resolve. Actually, whether or not one undertakes a fifth step in this practice of prayer, the fruits of genuine contemplatio will always eventually be felt in one's self-transformation into a deeper conformity to Christ.

When this step is added to the steps discussed above, the one facing cancer might resolve to face more honestly the implications of the illness. This could change one's manner of interacting with doctors, colleagues, friends, and family members. One might change one's plans for the future. These changes could be concrete or attitudinal.

Lectio Divina in Groups

Finally, lectio divina can be practiced in a group. Some of the steps lend themselves to communal engagement more than others. The size of the group will also influence the degree of personal involvement. The first step, lectio, or reading, presents no challenges. Slow and thoughtful reading of a biblical passage can be done quite easily in a group, regardless of its size. The insights gained from probing the meaning of the passage can be enhanced when done by more than one person. However, careful oversight should be practiced here so that no one in the group monopolizes the sharing. Before moving to the second step, relating the ideas and feelings found in the passage with authentic life experience, members of the group will have to decide what common experience they choose to explore. When the focus of meditatio is clear, insights from more than one person can enlighten all participants. Though this is a communal exercise with a common purpose, each participant will respond in oratio in an individual manner. Some might be moved to praise God; others will cry for help; still others will rest in confidence. It all depends on how the individual perceives the issue under consideration. Since oratio, which here is individual, moves one to contemplatio, the fourth step will also be an individual experience, although the shared silence and sense of resting in God may feel companionable and supportive. This process should assist the group to come to a communal decision regarding operatio if that step is included.

Lectio Divina and the Liturgy

The practice of lectio divina can bear fruit in many ways. It enriches one's appreciation of Scripture, as well as strengthening and deepening the individual and heightening individual awareness. The sensitivities and insights cultivated in lectio divina can also flow into and enhance one's experience of the liturgy. The words and images of the psalms heard or sung at Mass or in the Liturgy of the Hours will have new resonance for those who practice lectio divina with the psalms. The practice can be both an effective preparation for liturgy and a way of further savoring the psalms prayed in the liturgy.

FINAL REFLECTIONS

Life abounds with events that call for a moment of prayer in which psalms could be sung or recited in a group. This might include the blessing of a home or a car, a new educational or employment venture, the celebration of an anniversary or a birthday, or the sudden announcement of bad news or challenge. Furthermore, the versatility of the psalms invites us to recite them easily, chant them solemnly, or sing them joyfully at almost any kind of an occasion. Thus the psalms help to lace our lives together with the liturgy, increasing the power of God's Word in both settings. Since most human emotions can be found expressed in one or more of the psalms, in virtually any moment of our lives we might be prompted to pray: "O Lord, open my lips; and my mouth shall proclaim your praise."

FOR FURTHER READING —
A SELECTIVE LIST

Alter, Robert. *The Book of Psalms: A Translation and Commentary*. New York: Norton, 2009.

Bergant, Dianne J., CSA. *Psalms 1–72*. Vol. 22, OT of *New Collegeville Bible Commentary*. Collegeville, MN: Liturgical Press, 2013.

———. *Psalms 73–150*. Vol. 23, OT of *New Collegeville Bible Commentary*. Collegeville, MN: Liturgical Press, 2013.

Bruggemann, Walter. *Praying the Psalms: Engaging Scripture and the Life of the Spirit*, 2nd ed. Eugene, OR: Wipf and Stock, 2007.

———. *Spirituality of the Psalms*. Minneapolis, MN: Fortress Press, 2001.

Casey, Michael. *Sacred Reading: The Ancient Art of Lectio Divina*. Liguori, MO: Liguori/Triumph, 1996.

Harmon, Kathleen, SNDDEN. *Becoming the Psalms: A Spirituality of Singing and Praying the Psalms*. Collegeville, MN: Liturgical Press, 2015.

Lectionary for Mass: Sundays, Solemnities, Feasts of the Lord and the Saints. Study Edition. Chicago: Liturgy Training Publications, 1998.

Lectionary for Mass: Weekdays, Proper of Saints, Common of Saints, Ritual Masses, Various Needs and Occasions, Votive Masses, Masses for the Dead. Study Edition. Chicago: Liturgy Training Publications, 2001.

Magrassi, Mariano. *Praying the Bible: An Introduction to Lectio Divina*. Collegeville, MN: Liturgical Press, 1998.

Merton, Thomas. *Praying the Psalms*. Eastford, CT: Martino Fine Books, 1964.

Polan, Gregory J., OSB. *The Psalms: Songs of Faith and Praise, The Revised Grail Psalter with Commentary and Prayers*. Mahwah, NJ: Paulist Press, 2014.

Prevost, Jean-Pierre. Mary Misrahi, tr. *A Short Dictionary of the Psalms*. Collegeville, MN: Liturgical Press, 1997.

Schaefer, Konrad, OSB. *Psalms*. Edited by David W. Cotter. Berit Olam Studies in Hebrew Narrative and Poetry. Collegeville, MN: Liturgical Press, 2016.

Senior, Donald, John J. Collins, and Mary Ann Getty, eds. *The Catholic Study Bible*. 3rd ed. New York: Oxford University Press, 2016.

About the Cover Art

This is a detail from a page of the St. Albans Psalter, created at St. Albans Abbey in the first half of the 12th century for the anchoress, Christina of Markyate, who resided nearby. The large initial B marks the beginning of Psalm 33 (34 in our Bibles). Christ sits in the upper part of the letter, making a sign of blessing with his right hand and holding a book in his left. The psalmist, in the lower part of the B, points to the lines he urges viewers to pray: "I will bless the Lord at all times; his praise always in my mouth." This richly illuminated manuscript is at the Dombibliothek (Cathedral Library) in Hildesheim, Germany. LTP is grateful for the library's permission to use two images from the manuscript in this book. Learn more about the St. Albans Psalter and see all of the illustrations at the beautiful website maintained by the University of Aberdeen: https://www.abdn.ac.uk/stalbans psalter/english/.